A PRACTICAL GUIDE FOR IMPARTING THE FAITH

A Practical Guide for Imparting the Faith

Comprehensive Catechesis

DAVID J. WILSON

ST PAULS

Alba
House

Passages from the New Testament have been taken from *The New Testament: St. Paul Catholic Edition* (© Copyright 2000 by the Society of St. Paul).

Library of Congress Cataloging-in-Publication Data

Wilson, David J. (David Joseph), 1967-
    A practical guide for imparting the faith : comprehensive catechesis / David J. Wilson.
        p. cm.
    ISBN 0-8189-0988-9
1. Catechetics—Catholic Church. I. Title.

BX1968.W55 2005
268'.82—dc22
                                    2005011021

Produced and designed in the United States of America by the
Fathers and Brothers of the Society of St. Paul,
2187 Victory Boulevard, Staten Island, New York 10314-6603,
as part of their communications apostolate.

ISBN: 0-8189-0988-9

Printing Information:

Current Printing - first digit	1	2	3	4	5	6	7	8	9	10

Year of Current Printing - first year shown

2006	2007	2008	2009	2010	2011	2012	2013	2014	2015

This book is dedicated with heartfelt appreciation

To Fred Doolen
Whose late night discussions always brought energy
and contemplation

To my parents
Whose decision to send me to Catholic Schools mid career
planted a seed that would one day blossom to make me
who I am today

To Sister Anne
Whose influence on an impressionable kid
was exactly what God ordered

To my wife and kids
Whose patience with me is more than I deserve

To all those involved in catechesis
Whose "Yes" to God allows others
to hear His voice as well

May God bless you as He blesses others through you!

Table of Contents

Acknowledgments

Excerpts from *The Catechetical Documents*: Reprinted from *The Catechetical Documents* © 1996, Archdiocese of Chicago: Liturgy Training Publications, 1800 North Hermitage Avenue, Chicago, IL 60622-1101; 1-800-933-1800, FAX 1-800-933-7094. All Rights Reserved. Used with permission.

Excerpts from *National Directory for Catechesis* Copyright © 2005 United States Conference of Catholic Bishops, Washington, D.C. Used with permission. All rights reserved. No part of this work may be reproduced or transmitted in any form without the permission in writing from the copyright holder.

Excerpts from *General Directory for Catechesis* copyright © 1997 United States Conference of Catholic Bishops, Washington, D.C. Used with permission. All rights reserved. No part of this work may be reproduced or transmitted in any form without the permission in writing from the copyright holder.

Excerpts from *Sharing the Light of Faith* copyright © 1978 United States Conference of Catholic Bishops, Washington, D.C. Used with permission. All rights reserved. No part of this work may be reproduced or transmitted in any form without the permission in writing from the copyright holder.

Excerpts from *To Teach As Jesus Did* copyright © 1972 United States Conference of Catholic Bishops, Washington, D.C. Used with permission. All rights reserved. No part of this work may be reproduced or transmitted in any form without the permission in writing from the copyright holder.

Preface

"Though 'the Church is more than ever alive,' yet 'it seems good to consider that everything still remains to be done; the work begins today and never comes to an end.' (*Paths of the Church* [Paul VI, 1964]: 117) This document [*Sharing the Light of Faith*, National Catechetical Directory for Catholics of the United States] is presented to the Catholic community in the confidence that, as in the past, the Holy Spirit will guide the Church in our land in its catechetical ministry both now and in the future." (*Sharing the Light of Faith*, 11)

Years ago, as a Director of Religious Education, I began working on a catechetical model to help catechists (including myself) to solve the problem of not reaching all of my students. (I took it personally if I was not reaching a single individual.) In speaking with many respected people involved in catechetics, and after researching all of the pertinent catechetical documents, a process began to emerge that I felt was comprehensive, wholesome and complete in its approach to passing on the faith. After working with this model I began to see how it could radically change the way in which I performed my role as catechist and for others as well.

In sorting out the ramifications, however, it became clear that there was a whole history that needed to be investigated. Exactly how has religious instruction been imparted for most of the people in the Church today? Does their experience color their view of today's educational models? Is there a way of affirming the past and building upon it? These were all questions that I began to deal with.

In looking at catechetical models dating back about a hundred years, it was strikingly clear that the Church has undergone an evolution in its teaching methods. The question now became, "What does our recent past tell us and where do we stand at the present moment regarding our goal of imparting a complete catechesis?" It was clear that we needed a rejuvenation of our current models to address today's concerns relating to both content and process. It was also clear that the balance of the two, process and content or method and message, needed to be maintained. The new model that emerged, in fact, was not new at all. It was actually fairly ancient, being given by Jesus Himself.

Great! Now we have a new, old model, created by Jesus that can maintain the balance of process and content, while reaching 100% of our students 100% of the time! This is too good to be true, right? Actually, it isn't! It is that simple, and it gets better than that!

In looking to implement this in our parish program, I began looking to see how others in the parish could help facilitate this model to be actively involved in our program. Suddenly it became evident that this model was applicable not just to our educational component but to the entire parish and worldwide Church as well. What follows is the culmination of much research, practical application and prayer. This model is one which will enhance any catechetical program, using any textbook or curriculum, for any age group, and even more, for the entire parish as well. This model will hopefully enhance our parish life and create a people who feel a part of the Body of Christ, who yearn to know their faith in Christ, express it fully in various forms of prayer and worship, pass it on to all of those around them, and serve as best as they can the rest of Christ's Body. This is the vision of Christ in which we are a part. My hope is that God will speak through the pages of this book and that we will better know, love and serve this God who satisfies our every desire.

Introduction

(This introduction was originally intended for catechists and those associated with catechesis. When I began to realize the implications of this model and how it could be used in the parish as a whole, I felt I needed to revisit all that I had written in order to make it applicable to everyone involved in parish life. Take what you can and apply it to your own situation, keeping in mind that the goal is to help us to better know, love and serve God and others!)

Many times in my teaching career I have seen the glazed over faces of students who couldn't care less about what I was presenting. If you teach long enough, you know the look. It's like a dagger through a teacher's heart. Many of us take it personally, as if the blank stare were really the students' way of telling *us* to wake up.

The frustrating thing for many of us is that the subject matter we are trying to teach them often is of utmost importance. Teaching the life of Christ, our personal salvation, and the path to heaven should be topics that our culture yearns to absorb. And yet these children of God stare into the great unknown as if the heavens are not just beyond the veil.

At other times, you would think that we were on a different plane (or planet) than those with whom we share our stories. We try our best to bring them up to our level but they are drawn down as if by some unknown force. Our frustrations are born of a desire to communicate our understanding of an intangible love that the students cannot yet begin to see and feel.

These experiences are real and common. But many times the solution to the problem is simpler than we realize. This book will attempt to look at one of the most common hurdles in contemporary religious instruction and give a simple, straightforward solution that can be implemented and adapted to fit any style of instruction, age-level, curriculum or textbook being used. In fact, it is Christ's own method. So get ready to journey with me as we break open the Comprehensive Catechetical Model.

Our journey will begin by looking at our contemporary understanding of the role of religious instruction and the methods we currently employ. We will look at how Jesus modeled for us a method of sharing that we are called to use today. Next we will examine how this process actually complements, and is not in conflict with, the content we are sharing. Then we will break open each component of the process and look at how we can implement these methods in our current instruction, providing some tools on how to implement them. Finally we will ask the question, "So what?" and see if we can answer it for ourselves as well as for our students. Then we will discuss the ways in which we might see immediate results within our classes. We will then look at two factors that will impact the method: the catechist and the students. Finally, we will examine the ultimate goal of what we are trying to do as catechists, and ways in which we can accomplish them.

My hope is that teachers will have some fun and gain some practical ways to enhance and improve upon their mission in Christ. Jesus has called us to a most important role as Catechists. Let Him now teach us how to fulfill this calling by utilizing the methods He has given us to preach the message. Faith may be a gift from God; nurturing it is our gift to Him.

I am happy you are joining with me on this journey. May your trip be fruitful, and may the effort be worthwhile. God bless!

Prayer Before Reading This Book

(This prayer should be read each time you pick up this book to read.)

Heavenly Father,
You have gifted us with faith.
As we contemplate Your call to service,
give us the courage to respond as You will.
Bless the work of our hands
and help us to do it in Your most holy name.
May we be open
to know You more fully,
love You more deeply,
and yearn to serve You in others.
Forgive our weaknesses
and help us to be empowered to do Your work.
Send Your Holy Spirit upon Your servants
who follow in Your steps each day.
May we always be guided by Your hand,
and may we be happy to do Your bidding.
We ask this through Your Son, Jesus Christ.
Amen.

A PRACTICAL GUIDE FOR IMPARTING THE FAITH

Chapter 1

Contemporary
Christian
Catechesis

And, behold, two of them were traveling the same day to a village seven miles away from Jerusalem named Emmaus, talking to each other about all these events. And it happened while they were talking and discussing these things that Jesus himself approached and began to walk with them, but their eyes were kept from recognizing him. So he said to them, "What are these words you're exchanging with each other as you walk?" They stopped, gloomily, and in answer one named Cleopas said to him, "Are you the only person staying in Jerusalem who's unaware of the things that have happened there in these days?" "What things?" he said. So they told him, "Those concerning Jesus of Nazareth, who was a prophet mighty in word and deed before God and all the people, how the chief priests and our rulers handed him over to a sentence of death and had him crucified. We were hoping that he was the one who was coming to liberate Israel, but with all these things it's now the third day since this happened. Moreover, some women from among us have amazed us. They were at the tomb early in the morning and didn't find his body, and they came and said they'd even seen a vision of angels, who said he was alive. Some of those with us went off to the tomb, and they, too, found it just as the women said, but they didn't see him." He said to them, "How dense you are, and how slow of heart to believe all the prophets said! Didn't the Messiah have to suffer all these things and enter into his glory?" And starting from Moses and all the prophets he interpreted for them what was in all the Scriptures about himself.

They were approaching the village to which they were traveling, and when he made as if to travel further they urged him and said, "Stay with us, because it's near evening and the day has already come to a close." So he went in to stay with them. And it happened that when he reclined at table with them he took the bread and blessed it, broke it, and gave it to them. Then their eyes were opened and they recognized him, and he disappeared from them. And they said to each other, "Weren't our hearts burning within us while he spoke to us on the road, as he opened up the Scriptures to us?" They got up and returned to Jerusalem that very hour, and they found the Eleven and those with them gathered together, who said, "The Lord has really risen and has been seen by Simon!" Then they related what had happened on the road, and how they recognized him in the breaking of the bread.   Luke 24:13-35

Rabbouni! This phrase taken from the Gospel of John (20:16) is the only phrase I can use in referring to Jesus after having read the story about the Lord's post-resurrection appearance to Mary Magdalene. "Rabbouni" means "teacher" or better, "Dear teacher!" Jesus, our teacher, takes us in the above cited story about the two disciples on the road to Emmaus through the process of catechesis in one short journey. Just what is this process? And how can we model it? That will be the focus of this book. Welcome! I am happy to have you on the journey with me.

What a great story! This model of sharing is two thousand years old, and yet we are still trying to understand it to this very day! The Scriptures give us all the training we need. We must simply apply these to our times and let God guide our steps. Although there is much more to this Scripture passage than first meets the eye, we will leave those points for now and revisit them later. This story does however, set the stage for us in analyzing the learning praxis.[1]

It is important, right at the outset, to point out that in the Emmaus story, Jesus joined the two as they walked along and began to question them regarding their present concerns. He did not rush in and begin to preach to them His saving message. His role was to understand them first. He wanted to know where they were coming from and how they understood the recent events in Jerusalem. In so doing, as an excellent teacher, Jesus was laying the foundation for a great learning experience. Dialogue is a two-way street and Jesus listened to the two disciples as a mother listens to her injured child. Before a doctor can begin to heal, he must build a level of trust with his patient. And so, the learning process begins long before the teaching starts.

---

[1] *Praxis* is defined as a practical application or exercise of a branch of learning, or a habitual or established practice or custom, as defined by the *American Heritage Dictionary*, 1985. For our purposes, praxis will be referred to as the catechetical learning model used in Christian formation of the Catholic Faith.

Once the disciples have shared their stories, Jesus begins to unfold the meaning of all that has happened in the light of Scripture. Jesus shows them why they needn't be disheartened by showing them how Scripture had predicted all that had happened. Jesus begins to turn their sorrow into hope, their despondence into understanding. He gently leads them to a plateau primed for true sharing. In fact, He does such a great job that they don't want to let Him go. They reach their destination and Jesus gave the impression that He was going on farther. They had to stop, but they wanted more.

We, too, must always remember to be conscious of the people we are sharing our learning experience with. This is true of the smallest child to the most senior adult. We must know who they are, where they are coming from and why they are here, before we begin to share with them the "what" of the message when they are in our midst. This book will try to share the "how's," but we must keep in mind that these fellow pilgrims are people God has placed before us so that together we can come to know, love and grow in our Catholic faith. They are just as much a part of our journey as we are of theirs.

Catechesis, or the process of sharing the faith tradition, has undergone a series of evolutionary changes in the last one hundred years. In our lifetime, we have seen many different models of teaching that have shaped and influenced how we, as faith-filled people, attempt to share our understanding of God and His love with our brothers and sisters on the journey. Before we begin to look at the concept of a contemporary learning praxis, we need to be aware of our recent past history and to appreciate where we, our Church, the adults in our community, and our pastors have come from in order to better understand our current situation.

Sharing faith is a very personal experience. We therefore need to know ourselves in depth to engage in this process. Looking at how we were formed will give us a view into the methods and models that we have subconsciously made our own. This understanding will put into perspective our religious experience and help us to better journey with those around us. Just as Jesus entered into the journey of the two disciples on the road to Emmaus, we must enter into the spiritual journey of all of those people with whom we come in contact. Let us now look at the learning models of the recent past and see how they both helped and hurt the process of faith sharing and Christian formation.

Models of learning before the Second Vatican Council were more or less based on rote memorization and head knowledge. The sphere of reference for many older Catholics included, almost exclusively, the *Baltimore Catechism*. For Catholics being prepared for the sacraments of First Communion and Confirmation, learning the Catechism was key. In the Introduction to *The Catechism of the Catholic Church*, "On Catechesis, Catechisms and Catechetical Directories," Michael P. Horan writes the following regarding this emphasis on the *Baltimore Catechism*, "One unfortunate outgrowth of its use was the popular equation of catechesis with the small catechism, leaving the impression that catechesis is for children alone and carrying forward the accompanying assumption that memorization of content could function as the standard for initiation into the community of faith."[2] It was almost an assumption that spiritual formation would come later or through another source, but that the students must first be prepared in the factual doctrines of the Church before anything else could be imparted. Similarly,

---

[2] *The Catechetical Documents*, Michael P. Horan, Introduction to the *Catechism of the Catholic Church*: On Catechesis, Catechisms and Catechetical Directories, p. 636.

the role of the catechist then was seen as preparing students for "The Big Test."

This model worked very well for giving students an overview of the vast teachings of the Church that were the result of some two thousand years of ongoing theological study. Many of these students to this day can still quote questions and answers from the *Baltimore Catechism*. This is as impressive as Protestant students today who can quote Scripture, chapter and verse. Imagine an English professor teaching Shakespeare by requiring students to know each verse word for word and where they appear in the play. This skill would be highly impressive but it wouldn't necessarily guarantee a love of the author or the work. Furthermore it wouldn't ensure a better understanding of either of them.

With the Second Vatican Council many aspects of our faith life began to change. Gone was the *Baltimore Catechism* and most forms of memorization of doctrine. The focus now centered on the conversion of the hearts of young Christians. Students were led to be impressed with the awesome love of God. They were urged to love God and others through lives of service. Service projects became the norm, and students were making crafts of every sort for the church, the community and for themselves. They were urged to think globally and, as a result, stewardship and service became the new catchwords. The learning model had become more emotional than intellectual. Success was based on the various expressions of love through projects instead of passing tests. As a result, many called these the "fluff years" because of the lack of doctrinal content.

While there is nothing wrong with either of these models per se, neither method in and of itself is what Jesus was teaching us in the journey to Emmaus. To focus solely on the head and neglect the heart is in conflict with effective catechesis, just as it would be to focus only on the emotional aspect to the detriment of intellectual instruction. As stated in the document *On Catechesis in Our Time*, "It is important to display before the eyes of the intelligence and of the heart, in the light of faith, the sacrament of Christ's presence constituted by the mystery of the Church."[3] Now forty some years after the Second Vatican Council, church educators are beginning to understand the importance of educating the mind and allowing opportunities for this to change hearts, which in turn affect our actions in service. The process of catechesis is "more than merely instruction about Catholic Christian beliefs, values, and practices."[4] As stated in the foreword to the *National Catechetical Directory*, "…the errors which are not infrequently noted in catechetics today can be avoided only if one starts with the correct way of understanding the nature and purposes of catechesis and also the truths which are to be taught by it, with due account being taken of those to whom catechesis is directed and of the conditions in which they live."[5] Already we see the balance that must be achieved between method and message; process and content. Comprehensive Catechesis requires a person to share the stories of the church, begun by Jesus, who is constantly trying to form us into a community of love. The overwhelming failure in recent history is the failure to realize the importance of both process and content. The key for us today is to understand that, in Christian formation, it is the process that allows for the content to have an effect.

The root of the Greek word *katechein* is to "re-sound" or "re-echo." We are called by God to share once again His unfolding love. We cannot or should not do this in a cold manner. "The Church's

[3] *Catechesi Tradendae, On Catechesis in Our Time*, 1979, par. 29.
[4] *The New Concise Catholic Dictionary* by Reynolds R. Ekstrom, Columba Press, 1995.
[5] *General Catechetical Directory*, Sacred Congregation for the Clergy, 1971, foreword.

catechesis — and even more so, the catechist — must take into consideration all the human factors of a particular age level in order to present the Gospel message in a vital and compelling way."[6] Imagine telling someone that we love them without any emotion attached. It would be cold, bitter and worthless. But when we love someone so much that our desire to share our feelings cannot be withheld, then it is love that is on fire. It is God who has called us to share His love with others. If we have said "Yes!" it must be out of our love for Him. Anything else would be a waste of time and breath.

The story of Emmaus reminds us of this once again. The two disciples, after recognizing Jesus in the breaking of the bread, say to each other, "Were not our hearts burning within us while he spoke to us on the way and opened the Scriptures to us?" Jesus repeatedly shows us the way. In fact, when the two reached their destination, they begged Jesus to stay with them. Jesus had given the impression He was going farther but they pressed Him to remain with them. Imagine our students and parishioners pressing us in the same way! It is said that good catechesis always leads to "heartburn"! But how many of our students are ready to run for the door when the time is up for our session? How many parishioners rush for their cars to be the first out of the parking lots immediately after we have shared the Body of Christ? If this is your experience, you will hopefully learn some techniques in this book that will help to turn the tide toward a more wholesome, complete and rewarding learning experience.

Although this may sound idealistic, it is very easy to implement as long as we take a few moments to step back and look at

---

[6]   *National Directory for Catechesis*, 2005, page 187.

the whole picture. The reason that Jesus was so perceptive and insightful was in part based on His ability to see the "big picture." When Jesus predicted His impending suffering and crucifixion, Peter rebuked the Lord. Why? Simply because he did not have the foresight to see beyond his own sphere of reference. Countless times in the Gospels, people question Jesus with seemingly important questions only to realize how insignificant their thoughts were, simply because they were so short-sighted.

Our job as catechists and sharers must be to see beyond the horizon to where those among us must be led. In so doing, it becomes easy to design and implement sessions that help guide them step by step along the path of evangelization, a path that leads to a knowledge and love of God and of our acceptance of His divine will and plan. This is what Jesus tried to do on the way to Emmaus. As stated in the *General Catechetical Directory*, "Catechesis proper presupposes a global adherence to Christ's Gospel as presented by the Church. Often, however, it is directed to men who, though they belong to the Church, have in fact never given a true personal adherence to the message of revelation. This shows that, according to circumstances, evangelization can precede or accompany the work of catechesis proper. In every case, however, one must keep in mind that the element of conversion is always present in the dynamism of faith, and, for that reason any form of catechesis must also perform the role of evangelization."[7] Without following a carefully laid out process, our efforts seem ineffective because either those we are attempting to catechize didn't acquiesce or because the message was beyond their comprehension.

It is important to recognize the process that is emerging on

---

[7] *General Catechetical Directory*, Sacred Congregation for the Clergy, 1971, par. 18.

the journey to Emmaus. First, we see Jesus build a community atmosphere in which sharing becomes possible. He initially allows the two disciples to set the agenda about what will be discussed before He tries to show them "the way." In following His example we must find out where our students and adult group members are in their lives before we begin to answer their life's problems. Secondly, we find Jesus opening the Scriptures and explaining the present occurrences in light of them. We also must show how the Scriptures relate to our lives and problems. Only then can we begin to share our faith traditions with our pupils. After we have built a community of trust and openness, and have shown them how God is part of it all through the use of Scripture, we can show them how this faith is fostered, experienced, and shared. This is the third prong of the catechetical process and the core of what we do as catechists or sharers of the faith. This is the catechetical moment, the time when we share how the Church lives and expresses its beliefs. But, important as this is, if we begin this latter process before the first two, we are setting the stage for failure for many. Only after we are able to see as a people of God how our faith tradition relates to each one of us personally can we begin the process of acceptance with our hearts and minds.

As Jesus and His students approach the end of their session, Jesus gives the impression that He is going on, but they press Him to stay with them. Then they break bread together and the students recognize Him. This moment is so vital and moving that we can hardly comprehend what has happened. The recognition of Jesus in the sacrament of the Eucharist occurs only when the disciples have been led through a process that builds a community, evangelizes it, and teaches the faith of the Church through communion. It is through this process that people come to recognize Jesus in the sacraments and in all the liturgical celebrations in which we participate. It requires us to be formed intellectually and spiritually to be able to consciously participate and be actively involved in the various expressions of our faith. Otherwise, we are simply going through the motions as, unfortunately, many of our students, their parents and countless other parishioners are doing this very minute. It is through the light of Jesus and His revelation that we can see Him in the sacramental actions of the Church. This comes about through an evangelizing effort begun by God in which we are a part. Once we are able to come to a heartfelt acceptance of all that is taking place, we can embrace the liturgies for what they are: "The source and summit" of Church activity and prayer. This state of being allows all of prayer to be transformed into a fully spiritual event that embodies our entire being — body, soul, mind, strength. But our learning experience is not yet complete.

After the two disciples of Jesus recognized Him in the breaking of the bread, they didn't just go to sleep! They left immediately and traveled all the way back to Jerusalem to share with the "eleven and those who were with them" their encounter with Jesus. They were on a mission to share their stories of God. The model is now complete. After we have built a community, become evangelized and catechized, have shared liturgical and prayer experiences, we must accept our role in the building of the kingdom of God. This role includes activities of justice and service, of stewardship and acts of charity, and of performing works of mercy in Christ's name. To do all of the other activities without applying them to the Christian way of life would be fruitless. Not only are these required of us as followers of Christ, the process naturally leads to them. There is no way in which someone can have a full understanding of Jesus and His teachings without embracing Christian service. And so the Comprehensive Catechetical model concludes with providing opportunities for service and works of mercy.

Our goal as catechists of Christ is to bring about a radical transformation of lifestyle. In any culture and time, this would be a monumental task. One could argue that today's society poses as much of a challenge as any other. This holds the argument that the methods we use to relay the message are vitally important. Therefore we must constantly be prepared to do all that is necessary to impart our faith to those on the road toward Christ. Our bishops have recognized this challenge and encouraged its investigation. "Catechesis has to investigate new possibilities offered by the existence of the new technologies and imagine whole new models and systems if the Gospel message is to penetrate the culture, make sense to the next generation of Catholics, and bring about a response of faith."[8] It isn't enough to hand on the faith traditions. Our goal must be to inspire others to follow in the footsteps of Christ. In order to do this, we must explore every method available if it is to transform our culture. This new Comprehensive Catechesis is a way in which we may do this.

Methods of religious instruction have undergone extensive study in the past century. Our current understanding of how people learn has shaped the way catechists are beginning to teach, making use of contemporary catechetical models. The Church has been ever ready to use these tools to help catechists fulfill their call. "Indeed, studies have been undertaken with regard to the method to be used in the catechism lesson; the role of activity methods in the teaching of catechesis has been pointed out; the act of catechesis has been investigated in all its parts according to the principles which govern the art of teaching (experience, imagination, memory, intelligence); and finally, a differential methodology has been

---

[8] *National Directory for Catechesis*, 2005, page 16.

worked out, that is, a methodology which varies according to the age, social conditions, and degree of psychological maturity of those to be taught."[9] This being said, the model we witness on our journey to Emmaus is the same model that we propose today. Why? Because as human beings we yearn for community, we long to know God, to learn more about Him, to express our beliefs in ritual and tradition and to show our love of God through service to our neighbor. It is this model that calls us to better witness Christ Himself. And so this ancient, new model is complete. These five components of the contemporary catechetical model are:

> Community Building
> Evangelization
> Catechesis
> Prayer and Worship
> Justice and Service

If we can ensure that these five components are part of our program, we can guarantee that our program will be well-balanced, complete and wholesome. The model used in the Emmaus journey is the model that the Rite of Christian Initiation is built upon.

In the document *To Teach as Jesus Did*, our bishops outline a *three*-prong approach, stating, "All three aspects of the education mission are present, for example, in a well organized, comprehensive parish program of education where the teaching of doctrine supports and is supported by the building of community, and teaching and fellowship in turn support and are supported by Christian service through sharing spiritual and temporal goods with those

---

[9] *General Catechetical Directory*, Sacred Congregation for the Clergy, 1971, par. 70.

in need. In such a parish Catholic education's lessons are learned in classroom and pew; yet not only there, but also in the experience of living in a Christian community of faith actively engaged in service of God, Church and neighbor."[10] In the *five*-prong model outlined above, we choose *community building* as the basis or foundation, *evangelization* because we must make sure that all are properly disposed, *catechesis* to ensure the passing on of our faith tradition, *prayer and worship* to express our beliefs in an emotional way, and *justice and service* to express our love of God through our neighbor in need. In this journey Jesus is walking with us even if we fail to recognize Him. He is revealing Himself to us and helping us to know and love Him. Our hope is that one day all will recognize Him in the breaking of the bread and be led to share their stories with others. The echo will begin anew and we will continue the message of Good News begun ages ago, culminating in the prolongation of the life of Christ in us on earth, and continuing until His return in glory.

God has called us to participate in His plan of salvation. As baptized Christians we have a duty to fulfill the mission of Christ. By answering the call to serve as a catechist or adult sharer of the faith, we are being faithful to God. Let us never lose sight of the call of God and of the big picture. Our goal is to bring all people to know and love God. Hopefully, this will lead them to a desire to serve God as well. If we follow the example of Jesus we can accomplish all that God has in store for us. May God bless us on our journey!

---

[10] *To Teach as Jesus Did*, A Pastoral Message on Catholic Education, 1972, par. 32.

Chapter 2

Process
Versus
Content

Before the festival of the Passover Jesus, knowing that his hour had come to leave this world for the Father, having loved his own in the world, he loved them to the end. During the banquet, when the devil had already put it into the heart of Judas son of Simon Iscariot to hand Jesus over, knowing that the Father had given all things into his hands and that he had come from God and was now returning to God, he got up from the banquet and laid aside his cloak, and he took a towel and wrapped it around himself. Then he poured water into the washbasin and began to wash the disciples' feet and wipe them dry with the towel he'd wrapped around himself. So he came to Simon Peter.

Peter said to him, "Lord, are *you* going to wash *my* feet?" Jesus answered and said to him, "What I'm doing you don't understand just now, but later you'll understand." Peter said to him, "You'll *never* wash my feet!" Jesus answered him, "Unless I wash you, you'll have no share in me." Simon Peter said to him, "Lord, wash not only my feet, but my hands and head as well!" Jesus said to him, "Whoever has bathed has no need to wash his feet; on the contrary, he's completely purified; and you *are* pure, but not all of you." For he knew who was to hand him over; that's why he said, "Not all of you are pure."

After he'd washed their feet and had put his cloak back on he sat down again and said to them, "Do you understand what I've done for you? You call me 'The Teacher' and 'The Lord,' and rightly so, because I am. So if I, the Lord and Teacher, have washed your feet, you, too, ought to wash each others' feet, because I've given you an example so that, just as I've done for you, you, too, should do."   John 13:1-15

Whenever Jesus had a very important message to pass along, He always made sure that He impressed it upon His hearers in a very lasting way. In some cases, such as this, He even left them perplexed awhile until they could process the entire scope of what was being said. In this time-honored story, Jesus' message is service. The disciples must be of humble service to everyone. It's a simple message, and one that He could have easily relayed. The key for Him, though, was to make it stick. The disciples had to not only hear the message, it must somehow become a part of them, and a part of their new way of life. Jesus therefore chose to teach them in a new and different manner. He must show them, and He must do so in a very profound way. "Christ's method of formation was accomplished by diverse yet interrelated tasks. His example is the most fruitful inspiration for effective catechesis today because it is integral to formation in the Christian faith."[1] In the time of the Apostles, the washing of feet was a servant's duty. It was not something the master would even consider doing. So Jesus was teaching an extremely important principle. The message was vital and so the manner in which it would be imparted must be equally vital. Each gave weight to the other.

Many times in the history of the Church, we forgo this method of teaching. We are so concerned about the content of the message that we do not realize the importance of the process. Consequently, in recent years our focus on the process has caused the message to be underplayed. We are more than just teachers. We are catechists, sharers of faith. We are called to share our love of God. To do this requires much more than teaching skills. It requires that we balance the message with an engaging process. It means that the process cannot overpower the message. And it means that we cannot lose sight of the big picture.

Once again, Jesus gives us a new teaching model: live it, don't just preach it. More often than not, our example teaches more than our words. This is true in our teaching experiences, our personal lives, and in our Christian witness to others. As we journey with fellow Christians, we must realize that the journey in and of itself is also as important as the destination. If we don't portray this to our students, their enthusiasm will not be engaged, and we may do more harm than good. Creating lively, captivating lesson plans only enhances the message. It does not negate it.

Had Jesus simply told His disciples that they should be humble servants, some may have embraced it. Others may have simply forgotten it. Others may have just misunderstood its mean-

---

[1] *National Directory for Catechesis*, 2005, page 59.

ing. To model this behavior left a lasting impression on all who were gathered, especially since many of them already believed He was the Messiah. The important point for us to remember is that we must consider not only the message, we must also carefully choose the method in which it gets passed along. As many modern day texts explain, not everyone learns through the same styles. We must always seek to use methods of teaching that will engage our students while realizing that variety in teaching styles is vital. "God's own methodology inspires a plurality of methods in contemporary catechesis. The method or methods chosen, however, must ultimately be determined by a law that is fundamental for the whole of the Church's life. Catechetical methodology must exhibit a twofold fidelity. On the one hand, it must be faithful to God and to his Revelation; on the other, it must respect the liberty and promote the active participation of those being catechized."[2]

Passive teaching means that we simply pass along information in one direction: from the notebook of the teacher to the notebook of the student, often passing through the head of neither. This is the predominant model utilized in much of the twentieth century. The concept of "I am the teacher, you are the student; I talk, you listen" is vastly outdated. Sadly, this model is still widely employed. While there is a time and a place to use this method, it should not be the sole method we use. Active teaching, on the other hand, takes into account the people we seek to engage. It recognizes that there is someone and something else we must consider, that we must think not only about the "what" (the message) but also about the "who" (the students), and this will lead us to the "how" (the teaching plan). It means that we must look at the method as

---

[2] *National Directory for Catechesis*, 2005, page 94.

well as the message while considering the receiver. Oftentimes we do this without even realizing it. How many times do we think about "little Johnny" who will never be able to sit still through this lesson, or Sonya, who will have a hard time with this project? Through active learning, we engage the students as part of the process. They aren't by-products. They aren't lifeless sponges waiting to absorb whatever we throw at them. They are living, breathing, engaging, energetic, loving, and rewarding children of God. They are the sole purpose we do what we do. As we create lessons that are designed to explain the Good News of Christ, we must never forget these important points.

One factor that must be understood is that neither the message nor the method need be in conflict with each other. "Content" should not fight with "Process" for equal time. "Effective catechesis should feature no opposition or artificial separation between content and method… Content and method interact and harmonize in the communication of the faith."[3] This seems so simple that it shouldn't bear mentioning, except that this simple message frequently isn't adhered to. Very often, groups of people have chosen to pit message over method and vice versa. "Pope Paul highlights three areas of concern that are particularly apt for today's Church.… His observations center on preaching, mass media and the relationship between content and method in the Church's evangelization efforts."[4] This is the great debate that never had to be. Prior to Vatican II, the message or content seemed to take precedence over the method or process. Conversely, in the years immediately following the Second Vatican Council, we saw the process-oriented edu-

---

[3] *National Directory for Catechesis*, 2005, page 96.

[4] *The Catechetical Documents,* Thomas P. Walters, Overview of *On Evangelization in the Modern World,* 1996, p. 152.

cational models push aside much of the content of earlier years, much like a giant pendulum swinging back and forth. In the opening commentary to the document *Basic Teachings for Catholic Religious Education*, Jane Regan states, "Catechetical documents written through the 1970's recognize the need to balance the life experience of the learner with the systematic presentation of the Christian message."[5] Too frequently however, members of both camps feel the need to dominate the other. The people in the content camp battle with the process people and vice versa. This should not be a battle; it should be a dance. As stated in the document *On Catechesis in Our Time*, the International Synod of Bishops stated, "It is useless to play off orthopraxis against orthodoxy: Christianity is inseparably both.... It is quite useless to campaign for the abandonment of serious and orderly study of the message of Christ in the name of a method concentrating on life experience."[6] As sharers of the faith, we should work to balance the two principles and create a process by which the greatest number of students will come to a deeper understanding of the message we are trying to convey. After all, our message is the message of Christ. The method we use to share this message should be equally important.

When creating lesson plans, the point at which we start should be the theme. This theme should be simple, clear and measurable, although this last point will vary in degrees. The theme should be something which can be stated in a sentence or two, even if the explanations are much longer. For instance, if the topic for the day is the Holy Trinity, the theme could state: "Students will be able to define the Holy Trinity, who its members are, and how our faith is

---

5 *The Catechetical Documents,* Jane E. Regan, Overview of *Basic Teachings for Catholic Religious Education,* 1996, p. 118.

6 *Catechesi Tradendae, On Catechesis in Our Time,* 1979, par. 22.

built around it." Stating the theme this way allows you to measure if the students have grasped the concept which is easily stated by even very young students. The explanation of this concept is vastly greater than this theme, and the process by which we convey this message will vary by age, knowledge, and background.

Designing a process that will meet this goal is the next important step. In speaking about the reformation of the Rite of Christian Initiation of Adults, the bishops state, "The restoration of the process of initiation has itself prompted Christians to recognize what had been dormant for a long time: that initiation is not something that is merely learned. Its fullness comes from the experience of becoming a Christian in all aspects of human life."[7] We can easily research all there is to know on the subject matter and pass this along to our students, and, for some, this will be enough. But for the other students we need to do a little more work. We will need to look at other methods of teaching that will seek to engage students through various means. For instance, a student who is visually oriented might need visual aids to help illustrate the concept. Shamrocks and triangles are good visual aids in describing the Trinity. Kinesthetic learners may need to make mobiles or other craft projects to help them grasp the idea. Those who learn through interpersonal means may need to discuss with others the concepts given to them while intra-personal individuals may need time alone to dwell on what has been shared. Those who have a knack for music may need to hear a familiar tune that has been reworded to fit the concept of the Trinity. Many contemporary texts on learning styles will outline the various ways in which students learn and provide teaching methods that speak to these. The key here for us to realize is that

---

[7] *The Catechetical Documents*, Martin Connell, editor, 1996, p. 417.

we need to consider the manner in which we present the material, not just the material itself. We also must realize that neither is more or less important, or more or less demanding of our efforts.

As stated in the document *The Challenge of Adolescent Catechesis: Maturing in Faith*, "The fundamental process of adolescent catechesis involves discovering the relationships among the Catholic Christian tradition; God's present activity in the life of the adolescent, family, community, and world; and the contemporary life experience of the adolescent. 'Experience is of great importance in catechesis. Experiential learning... gives rise to concerns and questions, hopes and anxieties, reflections and judgments, which increase one's desire to penetrate more deeply into life's meaning' (NCD, 176d). In this process, Scripture, tradition and the contemporary life experience of youth are honored and held in dialogue. Adolescent catechesis encourages young people 'to reflect on their significant experiences and respond to God's presence there' (NCD, 176d). It enables young people to understand the meaning of their life experience in relation to the Christian faith. The Christian faith is a tool that helps adolescents interpret and test their experience; conversely, experience is a tool that helps them to understand the Christian faith. 'Experience can also increase the intelligibility of the Christian message, by providing illustrations and examples which shed light on the truths of revelation. At the same time, experience itself should be interpreted in the light of revelation.' (NCD 176d)."[8]

This may all sound a bit overwhelming and perhaps a little disconcerting. After all, many catechists are unschooled in teaching methods and most often unpaid. The thought of designing com-

---

[8]   *The Challenge of Adolescent Catechesis: Maturing in Faith*, 1986, par. 22.

pletely new and varied lesson plans seems like a major undertaking. But as our Church stated in the document, *On Evangelization in the Modern World*, "The conditions of the society in which we live oblige all of us therefore to revise methods, to seek by every means to study how we can bring the Christian message to modern man."[9] The process outlined in this book will begin to open a new way of sharing our faith for many that will hopefully flow naturally. Lesson planning will be left for a future topic. The issue for us here is to address the need for a standardized process that works for all ages and situations. How is this possible? It is possible because it is the human process. It is the process outlined by God and instilled in us as human beings who yearn to see His face. It is the sharing of His love echoing throughout history in the tradition of our faith. It is love begetting love. Practically the only thing you can give away and get more of in return is love, and God is love.

As we use the process outlined in Chapter One and emphasized in this chapter, we must always remember we are participating in the revelation of God Himself allowing us to know and love Him more each day. But as we participate in this plan, we must also consider the human person before us and the traits with which we ourselves are endowed. Humans have a need for acceptance and love. We therefore begin by building community. God is forever calling us to be happy in Himself and so we must explain how this life is filled with the glory of God. We do this through evangelization. If these two stages are properly executed, the human person will eagerly search to know more about this God of love, and as a result will look to worship and praise Him and to serve Him in and

---

[9] *On Evangelization in the Modern World*, *Evangelii Nuntiandi*, 1975, par. 3.

through others. And while the good news is great, it simply cannot be taught, it must be experienced. The role of the catechist is to share. You cannot teach about love; it must be experienced. Once this is achieved, we can begin to share true community in class, at home, and in liturgical celebrations with others of like beliefs.

One of the main goals as a catechist is to bring others to a better understanding and love of what we ourselves believe and hold dear. Sometimes, however, our desire to make this happen isn't enough. We must create an environment in which others can come to see and believe what we do. The process-oriented person must understand the eventual goal, whereas the message-oriented person must realize that as good as the message is, it rarely stands alone. When we take an approach that considers the message along with a method of presenting it, we are creating a total learning experience in the order of Christ Himself.

When we consider the people to whom we are preaching as well as the manner in which they need to hear the message, we will become much more effective sharers of the message. Priests understand this principle. Their homilies must fulfill these three requirements if they are to be effective: (1) Each homily must be based on the proclaimed Scriptures, (2) addressed to the community gathered before them in their current situation, and (3) must link the liturgy of the Word with the liturgy of the Eucharist. A priest cannot easily give the same homily to more than one community at any given time. The reason is that he must take into account the community gathered before him and the current situation in which they find themselves. This is true also of catechesis and the catechetical process. As we begin a new year of catechesis, one of the primary goals is to get to know the new students gathered before us, and to help them get to know us. This will help us to gear the message to fit their needs. For instance, this year's class may be more outgoing and participatory, whereas last year's class may have been more introverted and intuitive. Another class may already know a lot whereas the next class may need a basic refresher course. None of this can be discerned if we have not followed a precise method of catechesis in which we have journeyed *with* them instead of teaching *to* them. Besides, how can we share anything with someone we know very little about?

Many Church documents speak to the message or content. Publishers typically research these texts and do their best to conform their material to these guidelines. A special ad hoc committee of the U.S. Council of Catholic Bishops has been convened to review presented texts and to determine if they are in compliance with the teachings of the Second Vatican Council and specifically the *Catechism of the Catholic Church*. That being said, we will not focus too heavily on the content except to say that catechists should always be careful to make a distinction between Church teaching and opinion. Furthermore, catechists should also present the teachings of the Church in a positive and accurate manner. "Effective Catechesis... requires that the Church's teaching be presented correctly and in its entirety, and it is equally important to present it in ways that are attractive, appealing, and understandable by the individuals and communities to whom it is directed."[10] The document *The Challenge of Adolescent Catechesis: Maturing in Faith* outlines some basic themes that catechists should include. These are: Jesus Christ, Scripture, Church, Prayer, Action/Lifestyle, and Interpretation and Critical Reflection.[11] The document further explores these themes in detail and depth and gives a very good overview for helping middle to high school aged students.

---

[10] *Guidelines for Doctrinally Sound Catechetical Materials*, 1990, par. 69.

[11] *The Challenge of Adolescent Catechesis: Maturing in Faith*, 1986, par. 25.

By considering the people we are with on the journey, we are building a relationship. Jesus was a great relationship-builder. Everywhere He went, He immediately made a friend, simply because He didn't assume much about them. He saw in them their potential and their willingness to believe. The enemies He did make were people who rejected Him at face value. But He never let this stop His mission. If we are to be Christlike, we need to look at His approach to people and how He spread His message. Furthermore, we need to be open to allow God's Spirit to work through us as He looks to reveal Himself. We are co-evangelizers with God. This means we cannot do this alone and that God has chosen us to be a partner. Let us not debate the unnecessary, nor fight the useless fight. Our goal is to spread God's message, not our own. We therefore need to cooperate with Him in how this takes place, because only He knows the way to reach our students with the right message and the right method. Through all of this, we pray, may God's will be done.

Chapter 3

Laying the Foundation — Building a Community

"Everyone who hears these words of mine and acts on them is like a wise man who built his house on rock. And the rain fell and the floods came and the winds blew and beat against that house, yet it didn't fall, for its foundations had been set on rock. Everyone who hears these words of mine and doesn't act on them is like a foolish man who built his house on sand. And the rain fell and the floods came, and the winds blew and beat against that house, and it fell, and great was its fall." And it happened that when Jesus had finished these words the crowds were amazed at his teaching because he was teaching them on his own authority, and not like their scribes. Matthew 7:24-29

Jesus always loved giving practical advice. He knew you needed a good foundation to build upon and so He would often tell people things they already knew, but He would always bring it home in such a way that it would truly fit their lives. In a similar way, we begin our process by reminding ourselves to do what we already know. Before we can possibly begin sharing our stories with others, we must build a foundation of trust, caring, support, and openness. Those with whom we gather must believe that the facilitator, as well as the group as a whole, is a haven of mutual respect. If we want our students to be open with us, we must create an environment they know is safe.

Think for a moment about an important relationship in which you have been involved. The initial meeting make have taken place as a formal introduction, or perhaps by chance. Two people who are unfamiliar meet for the first time. Unconsciously, they may feel an urge to get to know the other better (or not!). This urge will guide their steps for a while so that they come to know the person more in-depth. This knowledge may lead them to like the other person a little better, which in turn, will cause them to want to know the other even more. This process of knowing and liking can result in a deepening of the relationship. If things go exceptionally well, the two may want to take the relationship to an even higher level, a lifelong commitment. This is a moment in which they accept the fact that this person is someone whom they know and like so much that they want to commit themselves to being available to that person almost at will. This natural process could result in a committed marriage relationship or a relationship between two individuals who realize that the other is a true friend with whom they want to build a healthy friendship. This is also the process God uses with His people. It is a relationship in which we gradually come to know and love our Creator more and more and willingly choose to serve Him in others.

This process involves not only the head, but also the heart and hands as well. And so, this is the process we will use to begin our journey toward God. In today's culture, we need to build a relationship with God just as we build relationships with others. Sometimes, people will need to meet God for the first time and come to know Him a little more over time. As we guide them to know Him more, we trust that God will do the rest. The crucial part for us is to have a good relationship with God that we want to share with others. It is as if we want to introduce our friend (God) to others who may not have met Him before. To do this we need to gradually set the stage for sharing by creating an atmosphere of trust and respect.

To create an atmosphere of trust, we need to be a good host. When we invite someone into our homes, or welcome them to a party, we want them to feel as comfortable with us as they do in their own family. It is therefore imperative that we put some effort into ensuring that our classroom space, the student dynamics and we ourselves are inviting and non-threatening. There are many ways to accomplish this, but the easiest and most obvious way is to respect each student as a child of God. The example we set for our students is vital in creating a class of model students. This holds true even for the difficult child in our midst. We must ensure that he or she is treated fairly and with respect. Our example should be that of Christian faithfulness and love.

Oftentimes students enter our class from many differing backgrounds and situations. Sharing our faith stories with them requires that we know something of where they are coming from. You cannot do this without entering into their journey and walking with them as Jesus entered into the journey of the disciples traveling to Emmaus. We must get to know our students as they travel along their way, but most certainly, they must get to know us as well. And as scary as this may be, it is our trust of our students that will lead them to trust us and each other.

"When day came, [Jesus] called his disciples to himself, and from them he chose Twelve, whom he also named apostles" (Luke 6:13). In the beginning of His ministry, Jesus formed a small community with His disciples. He chose men of various backgrounds, personalities, and gifts. These twelve men were to change the world with guidance from Christ and the Holy Spirit. I ask, is this much different from what we do today? We are blessed to share our journey with people of various backgrounds, personalities and gifts, and we, also, are to be led to change the world with the guidance of Christ and the Holy Spirit. And so, we must first build a community among those with whom we gather, so that they connect with us and with each other.

As the appropriately named document *To Teach as Jesus Did* states, "Community is at the heart of Christian education.... Men must be moved to build community in all areas of their life... if they have learned the meaning of community by experiencing it."[1] In the beginning of each year, our main goal should be to set the tone for the entire time our students are with us. The first few weeks are crucial in how they will acclimate themselves for the rest of the year. It is therefore imperative that we take these first few weeks seriously. Just as the foundation of a house is the most critical time of construction, the foundation we lay for the class is equally important. As expressed in the *General Catechetical Directory*, "In catechesis, the importance of the group is becoming greater and greater. In catechesis of children, the group helps to further their education for social life, both in the case of children who attend catechism classes together, and in the case of those brought together in a small number to engage in some activities. For adolescents and young adults, the group must be considered a vital necessity. In a

---

[1]   *To Teach as Jesus Did*, A Pastoral Message on Catholic Education, 1972, par. 23.

group, the adolescent or the young adult comes to know himself and finds support and stimulation."[2] We therefore come to realize the utmost importance of the group in catechesis. The group helps in facilitating the atmosphere and encouragement of each individual. Because of this, each individual has a vital role within the group. Each member has a certain gift or quality that lends itself to the dynamic of the whole. When someone is missing from the group for one reason or another, the group is lessened. Even when one person seems to be a challenge or an obstacle, their presence is crucial, because without them, the group is significantly changed. This is the Christian acceptance that we are called to practice in our lives, and it is important to model this within our classrooms.

Jesus Himself had some difficult students. Many of those who felt threatened by Him were constantly trying to trick Him up. Even His disciples were not model students. Peter rebuked Jesus several times, causing the Lord on one occasion to refer to him as Satan. James and John fought over where their place of honor would be in His kingdom. Thomas repeatedly needed direction. And of course, we cannot forget Judas. Even Jesus, the Master Teacher, had problem students. Could it be any different with us? The key is that Jesus never excluded any of them from His inner circle. He knew that each person is a child a God. Each person has a unique role imprinted by God, which means that each person is of value. This attitude is just as important for us. That is why community building is so essential in the beginning and throughout our limited time with our students.

As stated earlier, building community is as simple as being a good host. Ways in which we can do this are as varied as the hosts

---

[2] *General Catechetical Directory*, Sacred Congregation for the Clergy, 1971, par. 76.

themselves. It is important that we find ways in which we may accomplish the goal that is comfortable for us personally. To be honest, some people are better at building community than others, which proves the point that various gifts are given to different people. Many techniques that can be employed include ice-breakers, name games, small group exercises, sharing food, role-playing, prayer services, para-liturgies, and personal sharing. Keep in mind that, depending on age and personalities, no one community-building exercise will work for all groups. Sure you can try them, just keep in mind what your ultimate goal is: to build a sense of community of mutual respect, honesty, and affirmation. That is as simple as it gets. Christ wants all of us to love each other regardless of our differences.

It is sometimes hard to tell whether you have achieved any level of decent community atmosphere, simply because it is not that measurable. Our goal, and method, must be that of relational ministry. We really are not looking to measure much, we do however want a good atmosphere. Community building is a lifelong endeavor. When we model a Christian atmosphere within our groups, we could be setting a process in motion that will go well beyond the short time we have with our groups. We could, in fact, be fostering a future catechist or group facilitator in our midst. Similarly, if we do not do a good job of laying our foundation, we could be setting the stage for catastrophe. This lesson is one that I learned over time. I was not a great community builder by nature, but the value I have learned from these experiences has impacted my ability to teach far beyond what words can relate. It is not as if it takes a monumental effort, but it does require some.

Each individual in our classes is a vital person to God and us. Each one has gifts and talents that God has bestowed upon them. Each person is on the journey with us. None of them may stand alone. God requires that each person be interconnected so that we may strengthen, encourage, help, pray for, and love each other. We simply cannot complete this journey alone. Most importantly we cannot continue our journey without God. Someone once said that the greatest sin of all is not needing God. The second greatest sin is like it: not needing each other. Just as God is a community of persons — the Father, Son, and Holy Spirit — we must be a community of faith, hope and love. The community we create should be an example of the larger community of the parish. Our parish community should mirror the community of Catholic Christians, which should in turn fashion itself after the communion of saints. The community we build should strive to be heavenly, perfect, and Christ-centered. It should be a community that is blessed by God and led by the Holy Spirit, after which, the job we do in communion with God becomes easier and more fruitful. I pray that your community be solidly built upon the rock of Christ. May God bless your work.

Chapter 4

The
Framework —
Evangelization

During the high priesthood of Annas and Caiaphas, the word of God came to John son of Zechariah in the desert. And he came to the whole region around the Jordan, proclaiming a baptism of repentance for the forgiveness of sins, as it is written in the book of the words of the prophet Isaiah, "The voice of one crying out in the desert, 'Prepare the way of the Lord, make straight his paths.' Every valley shall be filled in and every mountain and hill brought low, the crooked ways shall be made straight, and the rough ways made into smooth ways, and all flesh shall see the salvation of God." And to the crowds that were coming out to be baptized by him he said, "You brood of vipers! Who warned you to flee from the coming wrath? Produce evidence of your repentance, then, and don't go saying to yourselves, 'Abraham is our father!' for I say to you that God can raise up children to Abraham from these stones. Already now the axe is laid at the root of the trees; any tree, then, not producing good fruit will be cut down and thrown into the fire." So the people questioned him and asked, "Then what should we do?" In response he told them, "Whoever has two tunics should share with the one who has none, and whoever has food should do likewise." Tax collectors came to be baptized as well, and they asked him, "Teacher, what should we do?" "Collect nothing more than what has been designated for you," he told them. Soldiers questioned him as well, saying, "What about us, what should we do?" "Don't rob or cheat anyone," he told them, "and be satisfied with your wages." The people were in suspense and were all wondering in their hearts whether John might be the Messiah. John responded by telling everyone, "I baptize you with water, but one more powerful than I am is coming, the strap of whose sandal I'm not worthy to untie; he'll baptize you with the Holy Spirit and fire — his winnowing shovel is in his hand to clean out his threshing floor and gather his grain into the barn, but he'll burn up the chaff with unquenchable fire." And so he proclaimed the good news to the people with many other words of encouragement.   Luke 3:2-18

As related in the Scripture above, evangelization is something that is initiated by God ("the word of God came to John") and is His way of preparing us to meet the Messiah. John went forth to proclaim the coming of the Promised One and to prepare the way for His arrival. Some preparation on our part is necessary before we can profitably meet Jesus. John, furthermore, tells us exactly what we must do: repent our sinful ways and lead a good life. After we have laid the groundwork for a small community, we must now encourage our students to become familiar with the Scriptures and evaluate their lives by them. In today's world, this is a real challenge. Many of those who join us on our journey come from harsh backgrounds. Many parents do not practice their Christian faith, and our culture doesn't help any of them. As our society more and more embraces secularism, we find ourselves constantly contending with relentless temptations toward consumerism, materialism and sexual liberalism. Our Church leaders are certainly aware of this problem. "In times past, the cultural tradition favored the transmission of the faith to a greater extent than it does today; in our times, however, the cultural tradition has undergone considerable change, with the result that less and less can one depend on continued transmission by means of it. Because of this, some renewal in evangelization is needed for transmitting the same faith to new generations."[1] The Scriptures, thankfully, are constant and unchanging. They hold high the bar of standards for Christian living and so we use them to help children and adults see what God expects of them.

Evangelization does not limit itself to setting a moral standard. The Scriptures are God's continual invitation to a deeper personal relationship with Himself. It is in the Scriptures that we begin to see for the first time and understand the immense and awesome love God has for His people. "Evangelization 'has as its purpose the arousing of the beginnings of faith.' (GCD, 17) ... It aims at interior change, conversion of 'the personal and collective conscience of people, the activities in which they engage, and the lives and concrete milieus which are theirs.' (EN, cf. Romans 12:2)"[2] Our use of Scriptures should begin to open a new world

---

[1]   *General Catechetical Directory*, Sacred Congregation for the Clergy, 1971, par. 2.
[2]   *Sharing the Light of Faith*, National Catechetical Directory for Catholics of the United States, 1978, par. 35.

for those who have no concrete understanding of God and also call them to evaluate their lives in relation to its message.

Our task of evangelization is a vital role toward Comprehensive Catechesis in imparting the faith. Evangelization looks to keep Christ as its center as we plant the seeds of faith. But of what does evangelization consist? "The Church's evangelizing activity consists of several essential elements: proclaiming Christ, preaching Christ, bearing witness to Christ, teaching Christ, and celebrating Christ's sacraments. (Cf. EN, no. 17)"[3] As we bring others to this Christ whom we have come to know and love, we are always conscious of where our focus must be placed upon, Jesus, the Word, who is Truth.

As catechists or small group facilitators, some of us may be asking, "Why are we expected to evangelize?" Because it is our role as Church to perpetually point to the "way." If people have gone astray in their own lives or been misled by their parents or friends, the Church stands ever ready to show them the true Christian way of life. Jesus always called people to better themselves and to live in God's light. "Jesus himself, the Good News of God, was the very first and the greatest evangelizer; he was so through and through: to perfection and to the point of the sacrifice of his very life.... To evangelize: what meaning did this imperative have for Christ? ... As an evangelizer, Christ first of all proclaims a kingdom, the Kingdom of God; and this is so important that, by comparison, everything else becomes 'the rest,' which is 'given in addition.' Only the Kingdom therefore is absolute, and it makes everything else relative."[4] It is through the use of Scripture that we show the true calling of each person of God. We have already es-

---

[3] *National Directory for Catechesis*, 2005, page 49.
[4] *On Evangelization in the Modern World, Evangelii Nuntiandi*, 1975, par. 7.

tablished that each person is of value through community build-ing. Now we will show how this value has its purpose in evangeli-zation.

The sacramental principle states that if we believe that God created the world and everything in it, then, potentially, anything God created could teach us something about Himself. The key for us is to be able to see with the eyes of faith. We need to work to see the glory of God in His various creations, including sometimes those within our midst. Mother Teresa was a great example. She made it her goal to see Christ in every person she came across, even the most difficult ones. Recognizing that God is in all helps us to see the world in a whole new way. It means that we can no longer condemn things (or people) out of hand, for potentially everything can lead us to God. As we struggle to live by this principle, the Scriptures provide the standard. Both for ourselves and for our stu-dents, the Scriptures are the key for our understanding of the ways of God.

The Scriptures also hold the key to solving life's problems. Jesus continually tries to convey the message that all we truly need is provided for by God. If we seek first His will, His lordship over us, all of life's necessities will be given to us besides (Matthew 6:25). The power of our faith is immense (Matthew 7:8, 9:22, 29, 15:28, Mark 10:52, Luke 8:25). God hears our prayers and will give us all that is for our greater good (Matthew 6:6, 18:19, 21:22, Mark 11:25, Luke 18:1, 21:36). There are many Scriptures that relate to all kinds of life's problems. There are many resources that help us to quickly find these passages when we need them. The important point is that we must begin to use Scripture to show others that we are not alone, even if at times it seems we are. We have a God who loves us, even if we feel no one else does. There is hope, even if there is no hope to be seen. God loves us so much that we cannot even fathom the immensity of that love. Our world desperately needs to hear this and it is our job to proclaim it. The unfortunate reality is that we are battling the whole world in many instances. But remember, Jesus has already conquered the world. The battle now is for souls, and so we must use every resource at our disposal and never give up the fight. Our job must be to lead others to the truth. This catechetical process will help us do this in a structured way that gently guides our students along the path to know, love and serve God in this world with an eye to being happy with Him forever in the next.

To evangelize must be our primary goal as a sharer of faith. Jesus stated, "Go into the whole world and proclaim the gospel to every creature" (Mark 16:15). Our mission must that of the Apostles and of the Church. "Evangelization is so central to the life of the Church that, should she neglect her sacred responsibility of bringing the Good News of Jesus Christ to all of humanity, she would be faithful neither to the mission entrusted to her by her Lord nor to her identity as mother and teacher."[5] Once our followers have come to know and love the Lord, the rest of our work is more easily accomplished.

One obstacle that as catechists and group facilitators we must confront is that many, many Christians today have not been properly evangelized. And yet, we attempt to catechize them as if they have been. We expect people to readily accept our message as if they are eager to hear it. The point is that evangelization is what prepares people to receive the Word into their hearts, just as John prepared the world to receive Christ. Community building allows for proper evangelization, just as evangelization will allow for proper catechesis. The Church recognizes this and has spoken to

---

[5] *National Directory for Catechesis*, 2005, page 67.

the heart of the matter: "Catechesis is a form of the ministry of the word that initiates Church members into the meaning of Christian signs and symbols. It is a ministry based on the assumption that the persons being catechized have already accepted the proclamation of Jesus Christ and are gathered by it into community. In practice, this generally is not the case. Too often, parish catechesis is directed toward individuals who have not consciously accepted the gospel proclamation. It is an attempt to catechize Church members still in need of evangelization. It was this very concern that prompted Pope Paul VI to address the need for the Church to proclaim more intentionally and more forcefully the love of God to all — both those outside and those within the Catholic community."[6]

How often have our programs throughout the world been guilty of trying to teach people about a God whom they do not know, much less love? How often do we expect people to fall in love with our message when they could really care less about it? You simply cannot expect anyone to love something (or someone) whom they do not know. So the process takes people from a perspective of knowing, then loving. It is through our use of Scripture that the seed is planted. "For in the sacred books the Father, who is in heaven, very lovingly meets with his children and speaks with them."[7] As we begin our process through community building, it gives us an opportunity to assess where our students and adults are in their lives. It allows us the chance to gauge where they are in their journey so that we can develop a plan to further them along. It is community building that allows us to do this, and it is our evan-

---

[6]   *The Catechetical Documents*, Thomas P. Walters, Overview of *On Evangelization in the Modern World*, 1996, p. 150.

[7]   *General Catechetical Directory*, Sacred Congregation for the Clergy, 1971, par. 14.

gelization that prepares the groundwork for our formation development in catechesis. Once again, our bishops recognize the problem. "Often, however, catechesis is directed to individuals and communities who, in fact, have not experienced pre-evangelization and evangelization, and have not made acts of faith corresponding to those stages. Taking people as they are, catechesis attempts to dispose them to respond to the message of revelation in an authentic, personal way. There is a great need in the United States today to prepare the ground for the gospel message."[8] Again, in each stage of the process we must "prepare the ground" for the ensuing step to follow.

You may have noticed the theme of house construction in the chapter headings for the Comprehensive Catechetical process. We recognize that in building a house, each component of the house depends and builds upon the rest. In our holistic catechetical models, we build upon each aspect to create a complete pattern of Christian formation. In community building, we lay a foundation on which everything else will be placed. In evangelization, we build a frame for the house to be built around. This framework must be completed based upon the shape of the foundation. We cannot expect every foundation to be the same just as we cannot expect every group of people — and therefore the dynamics within that group — to be the same either. Each group is different because each individual is different and the interaction between these individuals shapes the group as a whole. Understanding that every person is coming from a different place along their journey allows us the freedom and task to assess and configure a path that will guide them to their true Christian destination.

---

[8] *Sharing the Light of Faith*, National Catechetical Directory for Catholics of the United States, 1978, par. 34.

Catechesis cannot begin alone nor can it stand alone. Community building and evangelization are key to getting there. "But in the catechetical practice, this model order must allow for the fact that the initial evangelization has often not taken place. A certain number of children baptized in infancy come for catechesis in the parish without receiving any other initiation into the faith and still without any explicit personal attachment to Jesus Christ; they only have the capacity to believe placed within them by baptism and the presence of the Holy Spirit; and opposition is quickly created by the prejudices of their non-Christian family background or of the positivist spirit of their education. In addition, there are other children who have not been baptized and whose parents agree only at a later date to religious education: for practical reasons, the catechetical stage of these children will often be carried out largely in the course of the ordinary catechesis. Again, many pre-adolescents and adolescents who have been baptized and been given a systematic catechesis and the sacraments still remain hesitant for a long time about committing their whole lives to Jesus Christ, even though they do not actually try to avoid religious instruction in the name of their freedom. Finally, even adults are not safe from temptations to doubt or to abandon their faith, especially as a result of their unbelieving surroundings. This means that 'catechesis' must often concern itself not only with nourishing and teaching the faith but also with arousing it unceasingly with the help of grace, with opening the heart, with converting, and with preparing total adherence to Jesus Christ on the part of those who are still on the threshold of faith. This concern will in part decide the tone, language and the method of catechesis."[9]

---

[9]   *Catechesi Tradendae, On Catechesis in Our Time*, 1979, par. 19.

As we try to bring our students to a mature Christian way of life, it is sometimes difficult to remember the basics. It is helpful when we can follow a straightforward, structured program that helps us to stay on track. Furthermore, the background that we come from is oftentimes different than the background of others. By sticking to a structured method, we ensure that everyone will have the same understanding of where we are and where we are headed. We live in a new and different culture today than we did just a few years ago. The practice of religion and churchgoing are just two of many "choices" in life. Our young people today are coming from a place that most of us have never been. This process helps to overcome this. "In a time when so many young people remain untouched by the Good News, initial evangelization is a priority. Through evangelization we invite young people into the community of faith, into a faith relationship with Jesus Christ, and into the lifestyle of the Good News. Catechesis then builds upon this faith by explaining more fully the Good News and by exploring the common faith that binds the Catholic Christian community together."[10]

The community that we have built becomes a model of the larger Church community. This larger community has a vital role to play to our smaller community, and vice versa. We should all work and support each other in the ministry of evangelization. "Every task and every ministry within the Church is to be concerned with communication of the gospel of Jesus Christ to all peoples through the preaching of the word of God, the celebration of the sacraments and the living out of a life of love in the Holy Spirit under the guidance of the Church."[11]

---

[10] *The Challenge of Adolescent Catechesis: Maturing in Faith*, 1986, par. 9.

[11] *The Catechetical Documents*, Thomas P. Walters, Overview of *On Evangelization in the Modern World*, 1996, p. 151.

By living the gospel as people of faith and love, we are evangelizing. All we do in the Church should be done in the name of Christ. It should be geared to helping people to know, love and serve God and others. Can it be that simple? Were this the mission of every Catholic parish in the world, our focus would be clear and precise. If we evaluated every ministry with this mission in mind, we would clearly focus our intentions and actions on the most important aspects of our faith life. Knowing, loving and serving go hand in hand. They support and are supported by each other. The contemporary catechetical model is a way in which this mission is accomplished, with due respect for the ways in which we accomplish each in regard to age, knowledge, background, and understanding. "Shepherds of souls should always keep in mind the obligation they have of safeguarding and promoting the enlightenment of Christian existence through the word of God for people of all ages and in all historical circumstances, so that it may be possible to have contact with every individual and community in the spiritual state in which each one is."[12] We are simply called to minister to all people of all backgrounds and of all times. It is through the light of Scripture that we come to know and love the one true God. All else follows.

In today's culture, teaching the gospel is a challenge. Our great strength is the source of the gospel we preach, the Holy Spirit. While many in our world are drawn to a non-Christian or even an anti-Christian lifestyle, the gospel and the Holy Spirit are there to help us. Our goal is not to complete the task before us, but to contribute to it by working within the community framework of the Church. We are here to sow, or to cultivate, or to reap, but rarely to do ev-

---

[12] *General Catechetical Directory*, Sacred Congregation for the Clergy, 1971, par. 20.

erything, even in the midst of such great need. "Great numbers are drifting little by little into religious indifferentism, or are continuing in danger of keeping the faith without the dynamism that is necessary, a faith without effective influence on their actual lives. The question now is not one of merely preserving traditional religious customs, but rather one of fostering an appropriate re-evangelization of men, obtaining their conversion, and giving them a deeper and more mature education in the faith."[13]

We are joining a group of pilgrims who may not have a map, or supplies, or strength to continue. We discover travelers who may have no known destination or memory of where they came from. We meet travelers who might not have many skills or a desire to apply what they know. Then again, we may meet people who have a child-like appreciation for the forest they are in, who enjoy the company of those who are with them, and who love to share all they have. We are truly a rag-tag bunch, but we are all children of God, even if we don't always seem to know it. As we join the group, we bring with us the map and we know where to get supplies. We have a source of strength for the long haul in the Holy Spirit. We know where we are headed, aware that the past may have been rough and dangerous. We know that each person has certain abilities given by the Master. Our role is to enlighten, perhaps just a little, the minds and hearts of these pilgrims, so that they can come to see through our eyes the beauty, the wonder and the awe of this incredible journey called life.

---

[13] *General Catechetical Directory*, Sacred Congregation for the Clergy, par. 6.

Chapter 5

Raising
the Roof —
Catechesis

When he got out of the boat he saw a large crowd, and he was moved with pity for them because they were like sheep without a shepherd, and he began to teach them many things. Now when it was already late in the day his disciples came to him and said, "This is a desert place and it's already late; send them away so they can go off to the farms and villages and buy themselves something to eat." But in response he said to them, "You give them something to eat." And they said to him, "Should we go buy two hundred denarii worth of bread and give it to them to eat?" But he said, "How many loaves do you have? Go see." And when they found out they said, "Five, and two fish." Then he ordered them all to recline in groups on the green grass, and they sat down in groups of a hundred and of fifty. Taking the five loaves and the two fish, he looked up to Heaven, blessed and broke the loaves, and kept giving them to the disciples to distribute to the people, and he divided the two fish among them all. They all ate and were filled, and they filled twelve baskets with what was left of the bread as well

as some of the fish. There were five thousand men who
ate the bread.   Mark 6:34-44

Jesus always loved to give a really good lesson to His disciples. "Feed them," Jesus tells them. Jesus had already been feed-
ing them with His Word. It was late and still the people were hungry for more. "Us feed them?" the apostles thought. "But how?"
"We will do more than just *feed* them," Jesus replied. "Let us *fill*
them." And they were all satisfied. Better yet, there was plenty left
over after they had eaten their fill. As we guide our followers
through this Comprehensive Catechetical process, hopefully they
will become hungry for more and we will be able to satisfy them.
Looking at the big picture however, we know that there is much
that we continually leave out. There is much more to this faith of
ours than we can teach and share in the limited time we have. We
must trust that the little we have will be multiplied in the hands of
God.
     As we move through this catechetical model, we enter into
the next stage of catechesis. This is the heart of what we do as catechists. It covers every aspect of our faith lives and so, we now raise
the roof upon our framework and foundation. Since catechesis is
such a large part of what we do as we work to impart the faith to
others, we need to ask the question "what is catechesis, truly?" In
doing this we look to our Church to help define our task. "Catechesis
aims to bring about in the believer an ever more mature faith in
Jesus Christ, a deeper knowledge and love of his person and message, and a firm commitment to follow him. In many situations,
however, catechesis must also be concerned with arousing initial
faith and sustaining the gradual conversion to complete adherence
to Jesus Christ for those who are on the threshold of faith. With
God's grace, catechesis develops initial faith, nourishes the Chris-

tian life, and continually unfolds the mystery of Christ until the believer willingly becomes his disciple."[1] And later, "The object of catechesis is communion with Jesus Christ. Catechesis leads people to enter the mystery of Christ, to encounter him, and to discover themselves and the meaning of their lives in him."[2] It is catechesis that allows us the opportunity to fully develop that which we began in the stage of evangelization. In evangelization, we plant the initial seed that hopes to germinate into a hunger to know more about Jesus and His teachings.

It is catechesis that begins to deepen that which we have thus far only scratched the surface. "…The name catechesis [is] given to the whole of the efforts within the Church to make disciples, to help people to believe that Jesus is the Son of God, so that believing they might have life in His name, and to educate and instruct them in this life and thus build up the Body of Christ. The Church has not ceased to devote her energy to this task."[3] Being the heart of what we do, we realize its importance and we contemplate our presentation of this vital content. "Nevertheless, the specific aim of catechesis is to develop, with God's help, an as yet initial faith, and to advance in fullness and to nourish day by day the Christian life of the faithful, young and old. It is in fact a matter of giving growth, and at the level of knowledge and in life, to the seed of faith sown by the Holy Spirit with the initial proclamation and effectively transmitted by baptism."[4]

Catechesis is linked with the task of evangelization in that it allows the seed of faith planted in the initial proclamation to be

---

[1] *National Directory for Catechesis*, 2005, pages 54-55.

[2] *National Directory for Catechesis*, 2005, page 55.

[3] *Catechesi Tradendae, On Catechesis in Our Time*, 1979, par. 1.

[4] *Catechesi Tradendae, On Catechesis in Our Time*, 1979, par. 20.

watered and fed with the soil of the faith tradition that has expanded and matured over many centuries. Each step in this process is vital and must seriously be considered as we move along the Comprehensive Catechetical model. "Catechesis is so central to the Church's mission of evangelization that, if evangelization were to fail to integrate catechesis, initial faith aroused by the original proclamation of the Gospel would not mature, education in the faith through a deeper knowledge of the person and message of Jesus Christ would not transpire, and discipleship in Christ through genuine apostolic witness would not be fostered. Catechesis nurtures the seed of faith sown by the Holy Spirit through the initial proclamation of the Gospel. It gives growth to the gift of faith given in Baptism and elaborates the meaning of the sacraments. Catechesis develops a deeper understanding of the mystery of Christ, encourages more profound incorporation into the Church, and nourishes Christian living. It encourages discipleship in Christ and instructs in Christian prayer."[5]

It is important to recognize the work of God in this process. Our work is to be done with the help of God; sometimes God has to work in spite of us! Our role is to gradually unfold the articles of our faith in a way that holds to the truth and allows others to come to an understanding that takes root in their daily lives. "Catechesis should, therefore, assist in this cause (cf. UR, 6) by clearly explaining the Church's doctrine in its entirety (cf. UR, 11) and by fostering a suitable knowledge of other confessions, both in matters where they agree with the Catholic faith, and also in matters where they differ. In doing this, it should avoid words and methods of explaining doctrine that could 'lead separated brethren

---

[5] *National Directory for Catechesis*, 2005, pages 67-68.

or anyone else into error regarding the true doctrine of the Church' (LG, 67)."[6] It is interesting to note that we need to present other beliefs even when they disagree with Church teachings, but the goal is to show, in a charitable way, how the errors of those beliefs are in conflict with Church teachings. Catholic doctrine is forever stable, because truth never changes. We must always be careful to give a clear presentation of those false doctrines of the world as we show how they differ from what we hold to be true. "The case for Catholic doctrine should be presented with charity as well as with due firmness."[7]

In recalling how we are bringing our students and adults to a personal encounter with Christ, we must keep in mind that this process is generally a gradual one. We walk with people who are coming to a fuller understanding of God and who at times hunger and thirst for the fullness of God's love. This process must proceed with due care and consideration for the journey of each person. And while we build upon the successes of community building and evangelization, we realize that the journey is not a short or easy task. "Catechesis presupposes prior pre-evangelization and evangelization. These are likely to be most successful when they build upon human needs — for security, affection, acceptance, growth, and intellectual development — showing how these include a need, a hunger, for God and His word."[8] It is always interesting to follow the gradual maturity in faith of a person who is walking in the footsteps of Christ. In one way or another, humanity as a whole participates in this growth as members of the human race struggle to

---

[6] *General Catechetical Directory*, Sacred Congregation for the Clergy, par. 27.

[7] *General Catechetical Directory*, Sacred Congregation for the Clergy, 1971, par. 27.

[8] *Sharing the Light of Faith*, National Catechetical Directory for Catholics of the United States, 1978, par. 34.

come to a greater understanding of the meaning of our existence.

Aware that we live in a culture that is often in open conflict with our religious values, we realize that we must only adopt the influences of our society that affect us in a positive way. The sacraments, in making use of material signs to reveal a supernatural reality, teach us how to look for God in His created world. "Indeed, potentially at least, every instance of God's presence in the world is a source of catechesis."[9] Therefore we use the influences that are part of our daily lives to reveal the Creator as He invites us to know Him better. The content we present in our classes must, and can, be made accessible to our students in a variety of ways. "Catechesis reads the signs of the times — in our cultural values, in our lifestyles, in media, and especially music, and utilizes the positive values, questions, and crises of these signs. It challenges young people to reflect actively on the impact of these signs in their lives, and consider how the Good News relates to them. Effective catechesis is in tune with the life situations of youth — their language, lifestyles, family realities, culture, and global realities. It identifies the core meanings of the signs, symbols, and images of youth today, explores how these surface in youths' lives, and relates them to the signs, symbols, and images of the Catholic Christian tradition."[10]

Catechists differ from teachers in that catechists not only present material to be learned but they share their experience of how these truths influence their lives personally. Catechists, as witnesses, seek to express their experience of love in Christ. Having understood this, they use Scripture and life experiences to ex-

---

[9] *Sharing the Light of Faith*, National Catechetical Directory for Catholics of the United States, 1978, par 41.

[10] *The Challenge of Adolescent Catechesis: Maturing in Faith*, 1986, par. 23.

plain in a more concrete way how God is a part of every aspect of our world. "Like evangelization, catechesis is incomplete if it does not take into account the constant interplay between gospel teaching and human experience — individual and social, personal and institutional, sacred and secular."[11] Evangelization has led our students to an initial contact with Christ. Now, that relationship must be more fully developed. In catechesis we delve more deeply into the treasure trove that is our faith. "Catechesis is closely related to evangelization, which is the energizing core of all ministries."[12] Our catechetical work will more fully explain a God who previously was distant and unfamiliar. But catechesis is most fruitfully performed when evangelization has effectively taken place. "To put it more precisely: within the whole process of evangelization, the aim of catechesis is to be the teaching and maturation stage, that is to say, the period in which the Christian, having accepted by faith the person of Jesus Christ as the one Lord and having given Him complete adherence by sincere conversion of heart, endeavors to know better this Jesus to whom he has entrusted himself: to know his 'mystery,' the Kingdom of God proclaimed by him, the requirements and promises contained in his gospel message, and the paths that he has laid down for any one who wishes to follow him."[13]

The Comprehensive Catechetical model is a natural process that slowly and methodically leads the learner from the unfamiliar to the comfortable. It allows them to accept, on their own terms, the faith that we are attempting to pass along. By allowing each person to take his or her own steps along the way, the faith that

---

[11] *Sharing the Light of Faith*, National Catechetical Directory for Catholics of the United States, 1978, par. 35.

[12] *The Challenge of Adolescent Catechesis: Maturing in Faith*, 1986, par. 9.

[13] *Catechesi Tradendae, On Catechesis in Our Time*, 1979, par. 20.

they accept becomes truly their own. Although God (and we) are prompting and urging them along the way, we must realize that a mature faith is one which a person makes his or her own. The Comprehensive Catechetical model accepts this as a necessary stage. Each component of the model is a vital part of the whole. Catechesis — although the core of what we do as catechists — is a part of a much larger picture. "Catechesis nurtures the faith of individuals and communities by integrating four fundamental tasks: (1) proclaiming Christ's message; (2) participating in efforts to develop community; (3) leading people to worship and prayer; and (4) motivating them to Christian living and service (cd. NCD, 213)."[14] As we work through this process we are ever mindful of the final destination to which we are traveling. Our goal is a true acceptance and adherence to the Christian way of life. In order to come to this acceptance, individuals must feel that it is a choice that they are making of their own free will. "Catechesis has the task, then, of emphasizing this function by teaching the faithful to give a Christian interpretation to human events, especially to the signs of the times, so that all 'will be able to test and interpret all things in a wholly Christian spirit' (GS, 62)."[15] As we lead people to know and accept Christ, we are building a relationship that will flourish over time, a relationship that is and will be built around the truth and love of the Lord.

Any missionary traveling into a place in which they are to proclaim the gospel must prepare themselves for the task at hand. Through prayer and study, these missionaries equip themselves with all they will need to break open the Word to a people ignorant of the love of God. But more than preparing themselves with knowl-

---

[14] *Guidelines for Doctrinally Sound Catechetical Materials*, 1990, introduction.

[15] *General Catechetical Directory*, Sacred Congregation for the Clergy, 1971, par. 26.

edge and the skills necessary, there are some unwritten rules that they will need to follow in order to accomplish their mission. These missionaries must adhere to a number of societal norms that will allow them to communicate their message effectively. The truly successful missionaries of the past always did two things that enabled them to persevere in the face of great challenges among non-Christian people: they respected the culture they were encountering, and they spoke the language of the people they were evangelizing. These practices seem so obvious that they hardly require mentioning. But they are absolutely vital. By respecting the culture and speaking the language, these missionaries were able to accomplish a mission at which many others often failed. We must remember that those whom we seek to evangelize and catechize have their own culture and language as well. We must therefore be able to speak the language of the young people or adults we teach, as well as respect the culture in which they are immersed. "Catechesis, therefore, should convey the word of God, as it is presented by the Church, in the language of the men to whom it is directed (cf. DV, 13; OT, 16)."[16] The only way to do this is through community building. That is why this first leg of the process is so important. By casually becoming acquainted with any new group, we come to grasp the intricacies of what makes them who they are. It allows us to absorb those minute details that help us to more effectively bring others to come to know and love this God that we have long since accepted.

This gradual process is the same one Jesus used with the two men on the way to Emmaus. As we gently unfold the mysteries of God, our students will eventually come to an awakening when all

---

[16] *General Catechetical Directory*, Sacred Congregation for the Clergy, 1971, par. 32.

that we have shared with them becomes clear. This is the time when all of the little pieces of the puzzle begin to form a coherent picture that one can see and comprehend. "Thus through catechesis the gospel kerygma (the initial ardent proclamation by which a person is one day overwhelmed and brought to the decision to entrust himself to Jesus Christ by faith) is gradually deepened, developed in its implicit consequences, explained in language that includes an appeal to reason, and channeled towards Christian practice in the Church and the world. All this is no less evangelical than the kerygma, in spite of what is said by certain people who consider that catechesis necessarily rationalizes, dries up and eventually kills all that is living, spontaneous and vibrant in the kerygma. The truths studied in catechesis are the same truths that touched the person's heart when he heard them for the first time. Far from blunting or exhausting them, the fact of knowing them better should make them more challenging and decisive for one's life."[17] This is the moment when the process begins to pay off. This is when the metanoia moment — the moment of conversion — becomes the basis for going much deeper with our catechesis. In our journey to Emmaus, the two disciples realize that Jesus is in their midst. This is the time when our students thirst for more, and teaching becomes more joy-filled. For our adults, this is when their desire to accept and assent to previously hard to comprehend doctrines is made easy. This is the moment at which we may more rapidly unfold the rich history of the Catholic faith.

All that we have said thus far has been in relation to those who are in a formal program of evangelization and catechesis. Unfortunately, this is the mainstay of most parish religious educa-

---

[17] *Catechesi Tradendae, On Catechesis in Our Time*, 1979, par 25.

tion programs. However, if we refocused our efforts to reflect "Christian formation" instead of "religious education" we would see a need to retool our methods. Realizing that evangelization and catechesis are ongoing needs for the entire parish and worldwide Church will go a long way to renewing the faith of our age. This emphasis will also bring much more weight to the baptismal duty of all Christians to share the faith in their daily lives. This is the larger implication of the Comprehensive Catechetical model. But sadly, in too many programs, catechesis is left to be shared with only those preparing for the sacraments or in leading up to Confirmation. Generally speaking, catechesis is also performed by those for whom the title is given. "[Catechesis] is seen as a fundamental source of the Church's internal strength and external activity. It is seen as the duty and right of the whole Church, an activity 'for which the whole Church must feel responsible and must wish to be responsible'. *On Catechesis in our Time* makes it clear that everyone is in need of catechesis and that all are called to participate in this task."[18] All Christians must come to realize that true evangelism and catechesis occurs not just in the pew or the classroom but in the everyday life of each person. We share our faith by living it. As St. Francis said, "Everyday preach the gospel. If necessary, use words."

As we progress our followers to know and serve the Lord, we strive to attain that personal surrender to Christ that we have already given. Our journey has brought us before those whom we catechize. We seek to impart the faith with our fellow journeymen that we have accepted. If we patiently lead our travelers of faith to Christ, we will begin to share the journey alongside them, know-

---

[18] *The Catechetical Documents,* Thomas P. Walters, Overview of *On Catechesis in Our Time*, 1996, p. 369.

ing that our role is a companion (in every sense of the word). Literally, the term "companion" means one whom we share bread with. Those whom we catechize are thirsty for the Word and so we bring them to Him in every aspect of faith. "Catechesis attends to the development of all the dimensions of the faith: as it is known, as it is celebrated, as it is lived, and as it is prayed. It seeks to bring about a conversion to Christ that leads to a profession of faith in the Triune God and to a genuine personal surrender to him. It helps believers to become disciples and to discern the vocation to which God is calling them."[19]

Catechesis is a part of a much larger process of Comprehensive Catechesis that we have just begun to unravel. It encompasses all that we do and yet is not the end in which we strive. As we look to make "disciples" of all the world, we work in tandem with God to bring to maturity that faith that has called us to share our love for God. Catechesis covers all that we do in our Baptismal call to spread the word. "Every means that the Church employs in her overall mission to go and make disciples has a catechetical aspect. Catechesis gives form to the missionary preaching that is intended to arouse the first signs of faith. It shapes the initial proclamation of the Gospel. Catechesis assists the early examination of reasons for belief. It communicates the essential elements in the experience of Christian living. It prepares for the celebration of the sacraments. It facilitates integration into the ecclesial community. It urges apostolic activity and missionary witness. It instills a zeal for the unity of Christians and prepares one for the ecumenical understanding and mission of the Church."[20]

---

[19] *National Directory for Catechesis*, 2005, page 94.
[20] *National Directory for Catechesis*, 2005, page 56.

While catechesis is the largest component of the Comprehensive Catechetical model, it certainly is not the end of all that we do. There are still two components left to complete. The final two components are (1) prayer and worship, and (2) justice and service. The true end goal that we seek is for all of our efforts to manifest themselves in true Christian love and service. Catechesis is the means by which we get there. It is the vehicle that allows us to reach the goal. It is the roof that covers all that we do. Charity is our destination. "Catechesis, therefore, must foster and illumine the increase of theological charity in individual members of the faithful as well as in ecclesial communities, and also the manifestations of that same virtue in connection with the duties that pertain to individuals and to the community."[21]

As we travel to this destination let us look back and see how far we have come. Thus far we have established a firm foundation by creating a small community in which true sharing is a part. We began to open the Scriptures to shed light on the inner workings of the Creator. We have related our concerns, questions and problems to the Word of God. We have led our travelers to the deepest part of the forest by more fully explaining our faith traditions through catechesis. All throughout, we are conscious to share not just the "what" but the "why" as well. This gradual process allows our travelers to come to a more perfect knowledge and understanding of a perhaps formerly unfamiliar God but who is now a Person whom they have come to know and love in a personally accepted way. The last two components of the model will now lead us to the fruits of our efforts so far. Come, let us continue!

---

[21] *General Catechetical Directory*, Sacred Congregation for the Clergy, 1971, par. 23.

Chapter 6

Turning on the Electricity — Prayer and Worship

It happened that about eight days after he spoke these words he took Peter, John, and James and went up the mountain to pray. And it happened that while he was praying the appearance of his face was altered, and his clothing became a dazzling white. And, behold, two men were speaking with him, Moses and Elijah, who were seen in glory speaking about his Exodus, which he would bring to completion in Jerusalem. Peter as well as those with him had been overcome by sleep, but when they were fully awake they saw his glory and the two men standing with him. And it happened that as Moses and Elijah were leaving him Peter said to Jesus, "Master, it's good for us to be here; let's put up three dwellings, one for you, one for Moses, and one for Elijah" — he didn't really know what he was saying. As he was saying this a cloud arose and overshadowed them; then they were afraid when they went into the cloud. And a voice came from the cloud, saying, "This is My Son, My Chosen; hear him!" After the voice had spoken Jesus

> was found alone, and they kept silent and told no one in
> those days anything they'd seen.   Luke 9:28-36

Whenever we become involved in a new relationship, there is a period in which we spend time getting to know one another. In this period we try to discover things about the other to discern that person's character and interests. We may discover things about them that will change the way in which our relationship will develop. Oftentimes, as we get to know people, conversations revolve around seemingly unimportant topics. What becomes important isn't so much "what" is being said but the fact that we are spending time with the other person. It isn't so much "wasting" time as it is investing time. We invest in something that we hope is worth the effort. It takes a great leap of faith to willingly give up something of value, especially our time. It is this concept that leads us to the next component of the learning praxis, prayer and worship.

As we develop our relationship with God, there will come times in which our conversations with Him will be about seemingly unimportant stuff. At other times, however, our conversations with God will be about things that are vitally important. Just as we spend time in dialogue with others, we need to do the same with our Creator. God beckons us to know Him. In order to know Him better, we must invest something of ourselves that will lead us to know and love Him in a more profound way. And while prayer is the way in which we do this, it is catechesis that leads us to a desire to want to get to know more about this God and His ways. If we are methodical in our approach, sincere about our intentions, and faith-filled in our personal lives, this part of the catechetical model comes rather naturally. If we aren't, we need to develop a stronger relationship with God ourselves so that our desire to share is something that naturally flows from our teaching efforts.

If we have done our part well so far by sharing our traditions through catechesis, the adults or children with whom we have journeyed will have become a small community whose members respect and support one another, have come to see the role of God in their daily existence, and have come to a deeper understanding of the role of the Church and community in their faith-filled lives. As people come to know more about God and the faith in an authentic way, their assent will be one of a mature and confident commitment. As we continue to unfold the gospel message, our pilgrims will yearn to know more and want to develop a deeper relationship with our Lord. Through our example and the witness of our love, others will begin to realize the joy and happiness this life in Christ brings. As we guide them on the journey, we will introduce times and methods of prayer and worship that allow them to better cultivate their faith. It is as if we were teaching them how to fish and cook, instead of giving them a prepared trout almondine. We are in effect turning on the electricity to our faith lives.

Within our catechetical sessions, we share the faith traditions of our Church. We open up the wealth of the treasury of our faith and allow each element to become a part of the faith life of each individual. Part of the work we do in catechesis is to expose people to the ways and forms of worship through which our faith is expressed. One of the things that catechesis does is explain why we do what we do. It is in catechesis that the liturgy makes sense. "There is a close relationship between catechesis and liturgy. Both are rooted in the Church's faith, and both strengthen faith and summon Christians to conversion, although they do so in different ways. In the liturgy the Church is at prayer, offering adoration, praise, and thanksgiving to God, and seeking and celebrating reconciliation: here one finds both an expression of faith and a means for deepening it. As for catechesis, it prepares people for full and active participation in liturgy (by helping them understand its nature, rituals, and symbols) and at the same time flows from liturgy, inasmuch as, reflecting upon the community's experiences of worship, it seeks to relate them to daily life and to growth in faith."[1] The worshiping actions of the Church become the source of strength as well as a way in which the faith can be expressed in a tangible way. It makes the spiritual a reality. It gives emotional expression to our faith.

As catechists, we must always strive to share positive experiences of prayer with our students. In catechesis, prayer and worship are given flesh, and are no longer simply ideas that may previously have remained abstract. In prayer and worship, especially the Liturgy, we allow our students to give expression to the emotions that began to be tapped through evangelization and catechesis. Also, within our prayer experiences, catechesis is finally brought to fruition. "Catechesis both proceeds the Liturgy and springs from it. It prepares people for a full, conscious, and active participation in the Liturgy by helping them understand its nature, rites, and symbols. It stems from the Liturgy insofar as it helps people to worship God and to reflect on their experience of the words, signs, rituals, and symbols expressed in the Liturgy; to discern the implications of their participation in the Liturgy; and to respond to its missionary summons to bear witness and offer service."[2] In Comprehensive Catechesis, we include prayer and worship as we allow our prayer experiences to solidify every other component of the model. Each aspect of the model is so intricately connected that one cannot exist without the others and remain effective or holistic. As such,

---

[1] *Sharing the Light of Faith*, National Catechetical Directory for Catholics of the United States, 1978, par. 113.

[2] *National Directory for Catechesis*, 2005, page 110.

prayer and worship have always remained a vital component to catechesis.

Throughout its history, our Church has taught that prayer and worship are ways in which the Divine touches the human. "From its earliest days the Church has recognized that liturgy and cate-chesis support each other."[3] Prayer is the way in which our rela-tionship with God is fostered and deepened. Our worship provides an avenue for an individual's expression of love for God who is hidden. It is the human spirit's groaning for an intimate union with its Creator and Father. Catechesis prepares the way for this to hap-pen, and in doing so, brings each person to a desire to continue in their faith formation.

It is in prayer that God speaks to us. It is our worship of the Divine that tears away the veil that separates the physical from the spiritual. It is through this meeting of God and man that our eyes are open to the ways of the Creator. Catechesis, therefore, should unfold the meaning of prayer and worship so that each individual may come to an assent of the heart. "Catechesis should 'promote an active, conscious, genuine participation in the liturgy of the Church, not merely by explaining the meaning of the ceremonies, but also by forming the minds of the faithful for prayer, for thanks-giving, for repentance, for praying with confidence, for a commu-nity spirit, and for understanding correctly the meaning of the creeds.' (GCD, 25)"[4]

Having the "big picture" of our faith before us, we understand the value of prayer. Prayer is our source of energy in that it allows

---

[3] *Sharing the Light of Faith*, National Catechetical Directory for Catholics of the United States, 1978, par 36.

[4] *Sharing the Light of Faith*, National Catechetical Directory for Catholics of the United States, 1978, par. 36.

us the opportunity to get in touch with the Divine and helps us narrow our focus. Prayer charges our spiritual batteries enabling us to know and work within His will. Prayer is our compass that helps us to steer our lives according to God's design. Prayer is our spiritual kiss with God. It enables us to embrace our Creator and share our love with Him who satisfies all our needs. And finally, prayer is our emergency line for help in times when we desperately need forgiveness, support, and reassurance. The public and private ways in which we worship, adore, petition, give thanks, and ask for forgiveness are all ways in which God touches our lives. Mother Teresa said the following regarding the importance of prayer: "The fruit of prayer is faith, the fruit of faith is love, the fruit of love is service, and the fruit of service is peace."

By being prayerful people ourselves, we learn the art of expressing our spiritual yearnings in a concrete way. We are then able to share our experiences with others to help them to develop ways to experience the spiritual dimension of their faith. "Religious Educators then, who are mature in the faith, will teach prayer. This teaching will take place through experiences of prayer, through the example of prayer, and through the learning of common prayers. Religious education, at home or in the classroom, given by a teacher who values prayer, will provide both the instruction and the experience."[5]

Many in our world today are in desperate need of God's guidance. Too often we feel that our life is our own to do with as we please. While it is true that God has graced us with free will, our true happiness will come only from doing the will of our Creator. Our faith requires that we follow the path to holiness. Through the

---

[5] *Basic Teachings for Catholic Religious Education*, 1973, introduction.

various forms of prayer, we are strengthened and enlightened, we forgive and are forgiven, we intercede for others and ask for their intercession. Prayer and worship connect our faith and life. "Faith and worship are intimately related. Faith brings the community together to worship; and in worship faith is renewed. The Church celebrates Christ's life, death, and resurrection in its liturgy; it proclaims its faith in His presence in the Church, in His word, in the sacramental celebrations; it gives praise and thanks, asks for the things it needs, and strengthens itself to carry out its commission to give witness and service."[6] May we ever avail ourselves of these wonderful opportunities for grace. Our prayer and worship give honor and glory to God who bestows blessings and graces upon us. This cycle is renewed each time we glorify our God. He is only waiting to give us all that we need. We simply must ask for it.

We have thus far talked about the physical and spiritual dimensions of our human person. God created us in His image and likeness. If this is true, how do we resemble Him? If we accept the fact that God is one God in three Divine persons, Father, Son and Holy Spirit, is it possible that we are endowed with this Triune principle as well? If we look at the nature of God, we see the Father as the Creator, the Son as the Redeemer and the Spirit as the Sanctifier. Taking this further we can picture the Father as having the intellectual/emotional traits, the Son as having the physical traits, and the Spirit as having the characteristics of the soul. We can then look at ourselves as having three dimensions — physical, spiritual, and intellectual/emotional. By recognizing ourselves as beings with physical, spiritual, and intellectual/emotional characteristics, we come to understand the interplay that we must main-

---

[6] *Sharing the Light of Faith*, National Catechetical Directory for Catholics of the United States, 1978, par. 112.

tain between them in order to be fully in tune with our Creator. For instance, let us take the example of attending Mass. The spirit is always willing to do that which is perfect in the eyes of God. Naturally, our souls yearn to worship the Father and so our spirits are 100% into the liturgy. Perhaps we have dragged our bodies into church for Mass and are there physically. Is this enough? If we view this in relation to the triune creation theory, then we must also be in tune with the liturgy intellectually and emotionally. How often have we "been" to Mass but have not been to Mass? To participate fully requires us to be present physically, spiritually, and intellectually/emotionally. It is only in this way that we can ensure that we are offering our whole selves to the worship and glory of God. We now realize that our job of leading others to liturgy requires much more than just getting them there. It involves a complete offering of ourselves to the worshiping moment of prayer. "As members of the Christian community, all are called to participate actively in the liturgical prayer of the Church. Religious education therefore must involve the student in his faith community and in that community's liturgy."[7]

"The Church is a worshiping community. In worship, it praises God for His goodness and glory. It also acknowledges its total dependence on God, the Father, and accepts the gift of divine life which He wishes to share with us in the Son, through the outpouring of the Spirit. Worship creates, expresses, and fulfills the Church. It is the action in and by which men and women are drawn into the mystery of the glorified Christ."[8] Prayer and worship are essential components of the Comprehensive Catechetical model.

---

[7] *Basic Teachings for Catholic Religious Education*, 1973, introduction.

[8] *Sharing the Light of Faith*, National Catechetical Directory for Catholics of the United States, 1978, par. 112.

Just as each component builds upon the other, prayer and worship become the fruit of our efforts so far. Just as fruit requires strong roots and healthy leaves for food, strong branches to support its weight, and time to ripen, so our life of prayer requires a firm foundation and a nurturing atmosphere, a community to support it and time to bear fruit. Our Church has always seen the value of prayer within the community. It has steadfastly called its members to worship both for the glory of God and the building up of His kingdom. As we gather, may we be ever mindful of this call.

Chapter 7

Working on
the Inside
— Justice
and Service

When the Son of Man comes in his glory, and all his
angels with him, he'll sit on the throne of his glory, and
all the nations will be gathered before him, and he'll
separate them from each other, the way a shepherd separates the sheep from the goats, and he'll set the sheep at
his right hand and the goats at his left hand. Then the
King will say to those at his right hand, "Come, you
blessed of my Father, receive the Kingdom prepared for
you from the foundation of the world, for I was hungry
and you gave me to eat, I was thirsty and you gave me
to drink, I was a stranger and you took me in, naked and
you clothed me, I was sick and you cared for me, I was
in prison and you came to me." Then the righteous will
answer him by saying, "Lord, when did we see you hungry and feed you, or thirsty and give you to drink? When
did we see you a stranger and take you in, or naked and
clothe you? When did we see you sick, or in prison and
come to you?" And in answer the King will say to them,

"Amen, I say to you, insofar as you did it for one of these least of my brothers, you did it for me." Then he'll say to those at his left hand, "Get away from me, you cursed, into the eternal fire prepared for the Devil and his angels, for I was hungry and you didn't give me to eat, I was thirsty and you didn't give me to drink, I was a stranger and you didn't take me in, naked and you didn't clothe me, sick and in prison and you didn't come to me." Then they'll answer by saying, "Lord, when did we see you hungry or thirsty or a stranger or naked or sick or in prison and not care for you?" Then he'll answer them by saying, "Amen, I say to you, insofar as you didn't do it for one of the least of these brothers, you didn't do it for me, either."   Matthew 25:31-45

Our house is now near completion. We have laid a firm foundation, built a solid frame, covered the building with a sound roof, and have electrified every part of the house. We now begin the intricate task of working on the inside. This type of work is tedious, time-consuming and detailed. It means that we must get our hands dirty and work up a sweat as we take on this task to complete our project leading to full Christian maturity. In the Gospel story told above, Jesus is telling us as He has so many times the true essence of love. Once again, Jesus takes what we have complicated and makes it succinct and simple, yet profound. According to Jesus, the ultimate expression of love is giving of yourself, for "no one has greater love than this, to lay down one's life for one's friends" (John 15:13).

Love in its purest form calls us to service. It is this ideal that leads a man and woman to enter into a lifetime commitment of matrimony, which mirrors the marriage of Jesus to His bride, the

Church. It is this concept of love that led Jesus to the cross. And it is love that brings disciples of Jesus to willingly give their all to the cause of Christ. As we journey with young Christians to develop their faith lives to a mature love in Christ, we lead them to understand that love of God is expressed in our love for others. We cannot truly love God and hate our neighbor (1 John 4:7-21).

This principle calls us to live the gospel message everyday, in every moment. This is what leads us to establish our priorities in life and to act upon that which, in our view, is most important and in accord with the will of God. This is where the Christian works of mercy and the Catholic viewpoint of justice come in. "Christian educational ministry includes as a dimension of high importance the education of our own people to the imperatives of justice which should direct our national political, military, cultural, and economic policies."[1] Our Christian understanding of the faith and of the teachings of Christ are fruitless if they do not affect our everyday lives. It is imperative that we form our consciences by the Word of God and live our lives accordingly. Otherwise, the assent we have given is shallow.

As we work toward becoming more Christ-like, we will be amazed at the impact this has on our world. The ongoing battle that we have with evil in the world can only be won by our continual proclamation of the good news of God's love. "The greatest way the faithful can help the atheistic world to come to God is by the witness of a life which agrees with the message of Christ's love and of a living and mature faith that is manifested by works of justice and charity (Cf. GS, 21)."[2] The growth of the early Church was

---

[1] *To Teach as Jesus Did*, A Pastoral Message on Catholic Education, 1972, par. 26.

[2] *General Catechetical Directory*, Sacred Congregation for the Clergy, 1971, par. 49.

hastened because many people came to see in these new "Christians" a love that was authentic and service-driven. Even today, through the efforts of many service-oriented lay and religious orders, many people come to know God. It is through the witness of these Christians that Christ is reflected in the everyday workings of this world.

It is imperative then that any program that seeks to bring people to mature faith in God stresses the importance of Christian service and works of mercy. "Catechesis concerning justice, mercy, and peace should be part of the catechetical process. It should include efforts to motivate people to act on behalf of these values."[3] "Catechesis speaks of the works of charity performed by the Church and its members throughout history. It stresses that these works are essential and motivate people — beginning with the very young according to their level of understanding — to give of their time, talents, and earthly goods, even to the point of sacrifice. Catechists also present the lives of saints and other outstanding Catholics who have exemplified the Church's social awareness and desire to help."[4] It is through our catechetical programs and the experience and history of the Church in terms of works of mercy that we call our travelers to a love of service in Christ.

All opportunities for young Christians to experience the joy of serving others should be age-appropriate, a true expression of Christian love, and foster interest in doing the work of Christ. Children of the youngest ages can easily participate in activities that foster Christian love in action. By allowing even the youngest child

---

[3] *Sharing the Light of Faith*, National Catechetical Directory for Catholics of the United States, 1978, par. 170.

[4] *Sharing the Light of Faith*, National Catechetical Directory for Catholics of the United States, 1978, par. 170.

to help others gives them a sense of empowerment and appreciation for the well-being of others that no mere text could explain. It is through action that the true essence of our teachings take firm hold. By allowing all maturing Christians ways in which they experience Christian service means that we truly value the art of service in love. "Catechesis includes activities (involving vital contact with the reality of injustice) (Cf. JW, III) which empower people to exercise more control over their destinies and bring into being communities where human values are fully respected and fostered."[5] By showing people the needs of others around them, and by allowing them to serve them with love, we offer them a sense of accomplishment, increased dignity, and connection to those with whom we might rarely come in contact.

As we look to include this increased awareness into our programs, we should be ever mindful that Christian service begins in the home. As our families express concern for each other, they show that selflessness is a goal. When we stress the importance of love and care for other people, we lift the value of all human life. Our Church has always sought to lead the world by example. Our catechetical programs must therefore share in this goal. "Catechesis for justice, mercy and peace is a continuing process (Cf. JW, III) which concerns every person and every age. It first occurs in the family by word and by example. It is continued in a systematic way by Church institutions, parishes, schools, trade unions, political parties, and the like. This catechesis is an integral part of parish catechetical programs."[6] An unfortunate reality is that many homes

---

[5] *Sharing the Light of Faith*, National Catechetical Directory for Catholics of the United States, 1978, par. 170.

[6] *Sharing the Light of Faith*, National Catechetical Directory for Catholics of the United States, 1978, par. 170.

do not practice true Christian charity. It is therefore an essential role the Church plays in ensuring that all its members are shown the way in which to live our Christian lives. Many people have not been given a practical and living example of Christian love. The Church then fulfills its duty to "make disciples" of all the world by completing this process of a Comprehensive Catechesis.

"The experience of Christian community leads naturally to service. Christ gives His people different gifts not only for themselves but for others. Each must serve the other for the good of all. The Church is a servant community in which those who hunger are to be filled; the ignorant are to be taught; the homeless to receive shelter; the sick cared for; the distressed consoled; the oppressed set free — all so that men may more fully realize their human potential and more readily enjoy life with God now and eternally."[7] God graces people with varied talents and interests. We are called to use these gifts to further the kingdom and to bring the People of God ever closer to the will of the heavenly Father. It harms the body of Christ when we do not fulfill this call. When people use their God-given gifts to better themselves to the detriment of others, humanity as a whole suffers.

All of us are born as dependent creatures. We initially need others just to stay alive. As we grow, we become independent people. This is part of becoming a mature member of society. But our Christian duty calls us to be *inter*dependent, meaning that our lives are not our own. We must use our gifts to help others besides ourselves. This is the true calling of God. "Man, therefore, is called to embrace, in faith, a life of charity toward God and other men; in this lies his greatest responsibility and his exalted moral dignity.

---

[7] *To Teach as Jesus Did*, A Pastoral Message on Catholic Education, 1972, par. 28.

The holiness of a man, whatever his vocation or state of life may be, is nothing other than the perfection of charity (cf. LG, 39-42)."[8]

The process that we have followed in guiding others through the journey of Christian maturity reaches its culmination in acts of charity. It is love of God that gives us a love for neighbor, even of a neighbor whom we feel we should hate (read the story of the Good Samaritan). This love manifests itself in service; service to God and service to neighbor, using the gifts God has given. The catechetical work we have done up to this point has led to Christian service. It points to the cross that Jesus willingly embraced. Acceptance of our daily crosses is the fruit of the assent begun in evangelization and strengthened in catechesis. Appreciation and acceptance of one's Christian duty in the area of justice and service is one of the goals of our work as catechetical leaders. "Catechesis explains the relationship of personal morality to social morality. It makes clear that the Church provides principles which Christians have a duty to apply carefully to particular situations."[9] We shed light on the injustices of our world and allow the giftedness of each person to fulfill the needs of those who are injured by sin committed by others.

People who have righted wrongs are held in high esteem. The elevation of saints in our Church shows how much importance our faith places on good works. "Rooted in the Old and New Testaments and uniquely expressed in the ministry of Jesus, social teaching has developed throughout the Church's history."[10] God is love,

[8] *General Catechetical Directory*, Sacred Congregation for the Clergy, 1971, par. 64.

[9] *Sharing the Light of Faith*, National Catechetical Directory for Catholics of the United States, 1978, par. 170.

[10] *Sharing the Light of Faith*, National Catechetical Directory for Catholics of the United States, 1978, par. 170.

and if we are to be Christ-like, we must be a people of love. Love is a tricky concept. It means that we must persevere even if emotionally at any given moment we may not wish to continue. God is faithful, even if we are not. We must therefore be a loving people, even in the face of hatred. This is an all important task because "if you do good to those who do good to you, what credit is that to you? Even sinners do the same" (Luke 6:33). The Lord expects more of us.

Jesus said that the greatest expression of love is to lay down one's life for another. Not an easy task. Sometimes, however, it is harder to give our lives to another day in and day out in loving service. It requires a daily dying to ourselves. We do this by making ourselves available to our spouses, children, neighbors, employers, clients, and the stranger we may meet on the street. "Hence the importance in catechesis of personal moral commitments in keeping with the gospel and of Christian attitudes, whether heroic or very simple, to life and the world — what we call the Christian or evangelical virtues."[11] Jesus calls us to be readily available to every person in need, when convenient and inconvenient. This is the example He gave us. He was always ready to serve. His sense of being in the moment was key to His pastoral approach to everyone He met. He was never preoccupied with other things. We have a lot to learn from Him.

As we near the point at which our groups begin to appreciate their Christian duty, our role as facilitator is to guide them to a form of service that fits their interests and gifts. We may offer them a chance to help out in a variety of service projects so that they can discern where God may be calling them to serve. If acts of charity

---

[11] *Catechesi Tradendae, On Catechesis in Our Time*, 1979, par. 29.

and works of mercy are part and parcel of our lives as Christians, our Church should urge and encourage all people (not just those preparing for the sacraments) to eagerly participate in various opportunities to serve God and others. If serving others is much of what being a Christian is all about, we should be leading our people to fulfill this duty by using our time and talent to set an example. We are called to use what God has given us to bring about His will. His will is that we love all people: our friends, our enemies, and ourselves. Failure to do so makes our "Yes" to God fruitless, and as Jesus said, "Every tree that does not produce good fruit will be cut down and thrown into the fire" (Luke 3:9).

"What? Giving again?" I ask in dismay.

"And must I keep giving and giving away?"

"Oh, No!" said the angel, looking me thru.

"Just give until the Master stops giving to you!"

Chapter 8

So
What?

And, behold, a certain lawyer stood up to put Jesus to the test and said, "Teacher, what must I do to gain eternal life?" Jesus said to him, "What is written in the Torah? How do you read it?" In reply he said, "You shall love the Lord your God with your whole heart and with your whole soul and with your whole strength and with your whole understanding, and you shall love your neighbor as yourself." Then Jesus said to him, "You've answered correctly; do this and you will live." But the lawyer wished to find favor with God and so he said to Jesus, "And who is my neighbor?" After considering, Jesus said, "A certain man was going down from Jerusalem to Jericho and ran into robbers who, after stripping and beating him, went off leaving him half dead. Now a priest happened to be going down by that road, but when he saw the man he passed by on the other side of the road. Likewise a Levite was also going past the spot, and when he saw the man he passed by on the other side of the road. But a certain Samaritan who was on a journey came upon the man, and when he saw him he took pity. He went up to him and bandaged his wounds, poured oil and wine on them, set him on his own mount, brought him to an inn, and took care of him. The next day he took out two denarii, gave them to the innkeeper, and said, 'Look after him, and any additional amount you spend I'll repay you on my way back.' Which of these three, do you think, was a neighbor to the man who ran into the robbers?" The lawyer said, "The one who had mercy on him." Then Jesus said to him, "Go, and you do likewise."   Luke 10:25-37

Okay. We have learned the basic principles of the Contemporary Catechetical model. So what? What does this mean to us as catechists or adult facilitators? Isn't this the same question many of our students throw back at us just as we have completed a session that we have spent hours preparing? "Okay, so what? What does this mean to me?" Often this question is one in which the students have heard the message but they cannot see how to fit it into their own lives. Well, at least half the job is done! To be honest, this question shouldn't alarm us. It proves that at least the message was received. The goal now is to show how what we have taught is relevant to their lives.

The whole purpose of what we do is to bring people to fullness of life in Christ. While we work in tandem with God, we must recognize that there are many things beyond our control. A mature faith must be made on each person's terms. This is when we must surrender to God. God knows what is needed for each person to come to faith. The best we can do is to set the conditions that give others a clear direction in which to walk. "The fundamental tasks of catechists are to proclaim Christ's message, to participate in efforts to develop community, to lead people to worship and prayer, and to motivate them to serve others. To accomplish all this, catechists must identify and create 'suitable conditions which are necessary for the Christian message to be sought, accepted, and more profoundly investigated.' (GCD, 71) They recognize, however, that faith is a gift and that it is not ultimately their efforts but the interaction of God's grace and human freedom which lead people to accept faith and respond to it."[1] It is as if faith were a seed planted by God but which must be cultivated in order to grow. Although we prepare the groundwork to allow this to happen (a good environment, proper soil, the right amount of water, etc.), each person must give it the care, attention and time it needs to mature. While parents and catechists initially help the young to cultivate their faith, ultimate responsibility must be assumed by each individual. As catechists, we rarely like to relinquish control, and this area is no exception. But there is a certain comfort in letting go at this point. We have given our students the basics. Now they must learn to apply what they know.

A mature faith is one which a person has internalized and made their own. As we remain focused on the end goal, we look to the method that brings us there. We realize that a methodical process ensures an implanting of a desire to know the one true God in the being of each person. The Comprehensive Catechetical model gives us a way to bring the message into the heart and mind of each student so that they come to embrace that which we hold dear. We follow a systematic method that works for all people of all ages with any program. This methodology doesn't make the process cold and impersonal. On the contrary, this process is designed to allow for adaptation to work with a varied range of people, in age, knowledge and background. It is this methodology that allows for the content to be better absorbed. Realizing that our goal is to lead oth-

---

[1] *Sharing the Light of Faith*, National Catechetical Directory for Catholics of the United States, 1978, par. 213.

ers to Christian maturity, we need to be ever mindful of the people we are catechizing, which shapes the program in a variety of ways. The method, therefore, must be monitored throughout its use to ensure transition to each stage as the group develops.

Furthermore, the development of our program to uplift and make real our faith traditions requires that we show the meaning of the good news to each person. Our faith is universal to all people and for all times. Our task then is to continually reveal the role of Christ in the lives of our students. We do this by linking the Scriptures to our very lives. "Catechesis links human experience to the revealed word of God, helping people ascribe Christian meaning to their own existence. It enables people to explore, interpret, and judge their basic experiences in light of the Gospel. Catechesis helps them relate the Christian message to the most profound questions in life: the existence of God, the destiny of the human person, the origin and end of history, the truth about good and evil, the meaning of suffering and death, and so forth."[2] To do this requires much prayer, practice and patience. That is why we must maintain a balanced approach toward imparting the faith, in both message and method.

Balancing method and message is not something that comes easily. To say that both are equally important means that catechists must always put forth a concerted effort into ensuring both a fidelity to doctrine and an adherence to a methodology that allows the Word of God to infuse the soul of each person receiving it. "According to CT (*Catechesi Tradendae*), systematic catechesis is not improvised; deals with the essentials; is sufficiently complete, extending beyond an initial proclamation; and initiates the learner into the fullness of Christian life (CT, 21)."[3] All of what we do is useless if

---

[2]   *National Directory for Catechesis*, 2005, page 98.
[3]   *The Catechetical Documents*, Jane E. Regan, Overview of *On Catechesis in Our Time*, 1996, p. 369.

we cannot demonstrate how everything we teach, believe, practice, and share is connected to our faith journey. By following in the steps of Christ each day, we live in the joy of doing the will of our Creator, knowing that true happiness can only be found there. And so, every lesson plan and session we prepare must be completed by answering the "So what?" test. If we want our students to internalize our message, we had better give them a reason to do so.

We ask this question also of ourselves at this point so that we are able to focus all of our efforts. Why do we attempt to bring our students to know a God veiled in mystery? Why do we try to make them love this God who calls us to love without measure? What is the point of giving our time, effort and money to another person who may not deserve it or appreciate it? Why? We do it because this world cannot satisfy the yearnings of our soul. Only God can quench our desires. Our Creator alone gives us the peace that soothes a restless heart. We attempt to share an ideal that seems so illogical, but in reality, is the only true Paradise. So our calling is a precious sharing in the work of God, and we try to fulfill it in every manner available to us in the created world. "Since it is in a position to reach out to individual persons and groups, it is the 'privileged place' where 'catechesis is realized not only through formal instruction, but also in the liturgy, sacraments and charitable activity' (John Paul II, *Discourse to the Members of COINCAT*; cf. CL, 26-27; 61)."[4]

The emerging role of holistic catechesis will impact our Church for many years. Having reclaimed the model from the early Church, the Comprehensive Catechetical model, based on the catechumenate of the R.C.I.A., seeks to affect the whole person so that every aspect of their life is transformed to reflect the true na-

---

[4] *Adult Catechesis in the Christian Community*, 1990, par. 61.

ture of our creation. We struggle as a people to grow in faith. If our efforts are Christ-centered and oriented toward Christian love, each part of our being comes alive with enthusiasm and zeal. The efforts of liturgy, evangelization, parish life, social action and catechesis become avenues that point to the same path. When we are united in the same goal, our Church helps to bring humanity ever closer to perfection in Christ. Everything we do is vital to our mission. As we are able to streamline our endeavors and accomplish more toward our goal, every task becomes one which edges us closer to eternal life, a life that promises happiness and joy beyond our comprehension.

As stated earlier, this model which is based on the Emmaus journey, is the process used in the Rite of Christian Initiation of Adults (R.C.I.A.), the way in which inquirers are brought to full membership into the Catholic faith. All of what we have said so far is applicable to the R.C.I.A. as well as to all other catechetical and parish renewal programs. As such, implications of this model are far reaching. "The insights from the order of Christian Initiation of Adults have helped us to name that sacramental catechesis is not primarily about instruction in one sacrament but about forming us into a people aware of God's sacramental presence. Liturgical catechesis is not primarily a preparation for liturgical celebrations but an ongoing reflection on the mystery of Christ celebrated through the liturgy. This developed understanding is an essential component of contemporary catechesis."[5] As we question ourselves about the scope of our work, we are supported by the Church in our efforts and actions.

As leaders in faith formation, we have a duty to keep pointing to the path that leads to holiness. Is there more than one path?

---

[5] *The Catechetical Documents*, Jane E. Regan, Overview of *On Catechesis in Our Time*, 1996, p. 370.

Of course. Are there other methods that are available? Absolutely. The beauty of this model, however, is that it is adaptable to all people and all circumstances, simply because it is built around the group at hand. The only important rule to remember is that our mission is the same as that of Christ: a radical transformation of our lives to a heaven-oriented people. "Catechesis is not limited to one methodology.... Whatever the method, catechists are responsible for choosing and creating conditions which will encourage people to seek and accept the Christian message and integrate it more fully in their living out of the faith."[6] We keep our eyes focused on the prize as we walk steadily toward our goal.

The "So what?" test helps us to order our efforts to the most fundamental of tasks necessary to a full adherence of the Gospel message. By considering why we teach a particular session in a particular way we force ourselves to ground our teachings in the reality of life. "Catechists must be attentive to adapt their method of catechesis to the needs of particular groups they serve. Catechists serve a wide variety of persons, and the message of the Gospel must be proclaimed in such a way that they can understand it, and that it is applied to their life situation."[7] Every element of our faith has a concrete basis in reality. Part of our faith journey is to discern these meanings to each of us personally. Each group that we journey with shares its own unique reality of faith. Part of our goal as catechists is to discern this reality and bring it to the forefront of their faith journeys so that each element of the faith tradition is put into its proper context for each individual group. This sounds incredibly complex but is as simple as asking, and answering the question, "So what?"

---

[6] *Sharing the Light of Faith*, National Catechetical Directory for Catholics of the United States, 1978, par. 176.

[7] *National Directory for Catechesis*, 2005, page 229-230.

We see the model now in its context and realize its importance in the life of the Church. Having come to this realization, we now need to work toward implementing the model in our own parishes. In order that this model be effective, there are several steps that must be taken. Since this is a comprehensive model, we need to get everyone involved as we work together to achieve our goal. Our interconnectedness is what makes us "Church." As we orient our efforts to this process, we bring everyone aboard to journey with us. As such, we need to train all of our fellow catechists and facilitators into the workings of this model. We must ensure that each component of this model is thoroughly covered in the implementation of our programs. If our methods need to be adapted to allow for this, we do so realizing that this model does not conflict with any program, text or curriculum. Our pastors need to be briefed and fully on board, especially since this model includes liturgy, evangelization, and community building. Pastors must not see this as a threat to their pastoral responsibility, but a fulfillment of the baptismal call of all Christians. The parents, spouses and siblings of those in our programs also need to be informed about the workings of this comprehensive plan. Since this model is holistic, it is imperative that everyone who could possibly affect its development is not working in conflict with our efforts. Finally, our parishes need to be educated in the community implications. Our goal is to not only affect each individual or small group, but to impact the parish and larger Church as well. This model is intended to affect the world in which we live, and so beyond the work we do to implement this plan, we must pray, pray, pray. In both the beginning and the end of this book are prayers that are given to help us better transform ourselves and our world. As we pray for the guidance of the Holy Spirit, may we always work in unison with His will. I pray for you, that together our efforts fulfill God's plan.

Chapter 9

Seeing
the
Results

Now as Jesus was walking along the sea of Galilee he saw two brothers — Simon, who is called Peter, and his brother Andrew — casting a throw net into the sea — they were fishermen. And he said to them, "Follow me, and I'll make you fishers of men!" So they left their nets at once and followed him. He continued on from there and saw two more brothers, James son of Zebedee and his brother John, mending their nets in the boat with their father Zebedee, and he called them. They left the boat and their father at once and followed him.

Matthew 4:18-22

Jesus said, "Don't you say, 'There are still four months, and then comes the harvest'? Behold, I tell you, lift up your eyes and look at the fields, because they're white for the harvest. Already the reaper receives his pay and gathers fruit for eternal life, so that the sower and reaper rejoice together. For in this the saying is true, 'One is the sower and another the reaper.' I sent you to reap what you didn't work for. Others have labored and you are sharing in the fruits of their labor."   John 4:35-38

Jesus calls us to be fishers of men. In doing so, we cast a wide net and bring in all who are near to us. Fishing this way allows us to bring as many fish to ourselves as possible. Sooner or later, when the fishing around us begins to dry up, we may move to new waters and continue to cast our nets. Fishing like this is easy for anyone to understand and perform. This is not the type of fishing I am used to. I grew up in Southeast Louisiana. Fishing there was with rod and reel. You needed a boat to get out into open waters or to inlets and bayous that were not easily accessible. You needed all sorts of tackle and lures. You needed live or fresh bait. The fishing was good, but you also needed skill. After marrying, my wife and I moved to Southeast Tennessee, quite a ways from any salt water. Fishing there required even more skill and a completely different assortment of tackle and bait. Fishing was still generally done by rod and reel, but sometimes I even tried fly fishing. This required a whole different collection of gear; new rod and reel, new lures and new techniques.

The type of fishing done by professional fishers in Jesus' time and ours is completely different. It doesn't require much skill and the equipment is altogether designed for other purposes. The goal in professional fishing is to bring in as many fish as you can. Unfortunately you catch other things that you weren't intending to bring in. There are times when you bring in inedible fish (trash fish as we called them), sticks, seaweed, and other garbage from the sea bottom. You sort through this stuff with some effort, but it's worth it because the catch is much bigger.

The fishing we do in catechetical ministry is much more like professional fishing. Our goal is to bring in as many fish as possible and sort out the other stuff later. It requires a completely different set of tools than does individual evangelization and catechesis. It means that we must learn new techniques and to be in it for the long haul (professional fishermen often go out for days or weeks at a time). It is important for us to realize, whenever we go fishing, that there will be times when a few will get away in spite of our best efforts. Even, Jesus, the Master teacher (and fisherman), lost some (see Luke 22:48, Matthew 19:22, John 10:24-39 etc.).

As we approach our mission to bring the Good News to others, we need to realize that there will always be people beyond our reach. This is disheartening (especially for me!) because we truly desire to bring people to truth and happiness. Our frustration is the same as our Father's, but this doesn't mean we stop and give up. We always try our best, using every gift at our disposal. But when we are faced with a person who seems impenetrable, we must remember that even Jesus was incapable of changing the hearts of some. While it is true that faith is a gift, it must be nourished to grow. God plants the seed of faith in each individual. Every person has this gift. But if we want it to be strong and healthy, we must nurture it to maturity.

Having said all this, our efforts need to be as enthusiastic as if this weren't true. We attempt to bring all people to God in every manner possible. The Good News is a message for every person created in the image and likeness of God. When we assume the responsibility of sharing this news, we do so with the hope that everyone will embrace it knowing that this may not be true. And so we come to that point in our process when we take measure of our efforts so far. We look to see how everything we have done has been received and how this has impacted the people we gather around us.

Every person we come across has been shaped by someone before us. Even as we bring babies into the world, God has already molded them with His hands. The work we do then is part of a process that begins before us and ends after us. We truly reap what we

do not sow and sow what we will not reap. We accept the task before us and do it with joy and humility knowing that we are only
part of a much grander scheme in the landscape of God's eyes. All
of those we encounter will touch us as we touch them as well. Sometimes the impact we have on each other is profound. At other times,
it is subtle. Still, many other times, the impact others have on us,
or we on them, is one that lies dormant for a while until something
triggers its growth. It then blossoms to reveal a hidden treasure that
heretofore seemed nothing at all. Such is the effect we have on each
other. We are leading people to know, love and serve God better.
The seeds we plant in others are ones that will hopefully take root,
grow and bear fruit in ways we can never imagine. This being said,
what should we look for among our students to see if we are going
in the right direction?

There will be times when, traveling along, we come across
patches where the trees thin out to show us a vision of where we
have been and where we are going, and this allows us to assess our
progress. At other times the forest will be so dense with trees and
underbrush that it becomes difficult to even see the path. The key
for us is to continually look for signs along the way. Some of them
may be subtle, and others may be clear. It is important to recognize the signs for what they are and what they mean.

In terms of community building, we look for a sense of openness and sharing. This means that there must be respect for everyone in the group and a comfort level such that all present feel safe
to reveal things about themselves. "Catechists/religion teachers who
are capable of being vulnerable provide a tremendous support to
the adolescent, encouraging the adolescent's growth toward maturity as an adult. When the adolescent perceives a catechist/religion
teacher who is comfortable with personal limitations and capable
of admitting failure, the way is opened for the adolescent's own

personal self-acceptance."[1] Though one of the more critical stages in the process, it is often the hardest to measure in terms of its achievement. We try to measure it by testing the waters on a variety of levels. The comfort level we want the group to achieve varies according to the purpose and depth to which we want to take the group in our travels together. For instance, if we are traveling to the top of Mount Everest, we will want a group of people on whom we can count for our very lives, whereas, the group we are taking to the local aquarium doesn't need to pass the "jump on the hand grenade" test. The level we wish to achieve will also depend on age, length of time the group will be together, and how much sharing will be necessary. This is a tricky call and one in which experience and experiment will guide us. A buzz-word that seems appropriate is "relational ministry." We are attempting to build a relationship among the members of our group that allows us to achieve our end goal without involving us too much unnecessarily in each other's lives. This is truly a judgment call and one for which there is no clear answer.

In the evangelization stage, we again must decide to what depth we need to take our group. In most cases, evangelization will depend on the group and our destination. We need to give sufficient knowledge of Christ and Scripture to allow for a general discussion and investigation of the topics to be covered and for the gospel to affect their lives. Another buzz-word we should discuss at this time is "metanoia." This is a word that has been used to describe a radical change in lifestyle based upon how well rooted the gospel has become in their lives. For our purposes, "radical change" would describe a person who sees, understands and acts upon their

---

[1] *The Challenge of Adolescent Catechesis: Maturing in Faith*, 1986, par. 44.

understanding of the calling the gospel is prompting. Once again, this varies by age and level of Christian maturity. Keep in mind however, that "change" would be described as a measurable notice of an alteration in behavior. "This Kingdom and this salvation, which are the key words of Jesus Christ's evangelization, are available to every human being as grace and mercy, and yet at the same time each individual must gain them by force — they belong to the violent, says the Lord, through toil and suffering, through a life lived according to the gospel, through abnegation and the cross, through the spirit of the beatitudes. But above all each individual gains them through a total interior renewal which the gospel calls metanoia; it is a radical conversion, a profound change of mind and heart."[2]

Catechesis will take us to an area that is much more easily measured, which makes it a comfortable place for many catechists. Being teachers at heart, we want to be able to evaluate each individual so that we know how to change our methods and practices if warranted. Our contemporary understanding of the role of catechesis however modifies this a bit. Catechesis differs from teaching in that we become more of a "sharer" in the community than a "teacher." This makes measuring progress and fulfillment a little harder but still able to be accomplished. A later chapter will investigate this further, but the degree to which the group members take part in the discussions indicates the level of their commitment to this process. As the individuals in the group accept and understand their role in the formation of each other, they realize the importance of their participation. The catechist is a facilitator who not only teaches the facts about the faith but shows how these

---

[2]   *On Evangelization in the Modern World, Evangelii Nuntiandi*, 1975, par. 10.

facts should impact our lives as Christians. "Education 'does not merely strive to foster in the human person the maturity already described. Rather, its principal aims are these: that as the baptized person is gradually introduced into a knowledge of the mystery of salvation, he or she may daily grow more conscious of the gift of faith which has been received....' A Christian formation process might therefore be described as an organic set of elements with a single purpose: gradual development of every capability of every student, enabling each one to attain an integral formation within a context that includes the Christian religious dimension and recognizes the help of grace."[3]

Obviously, participation in group prayer and worship are measurable activities. Do our members desire to pray and worship because it is an expression of their beliefs or do they do it because it is expected or required? Forcing people to pray, worship, or receive the sacraments doesn't make them holier. In fact it demeans the whole process. We can do holy things all day without ever becoming holy. Once again, we look to our ultimate goal. What we are trying to do is bring people to a degree of Christian maturity manifested in their desire to get closer to God no matter what. As we begin to see our group members eager to pray, we know that we are on the right track. Incidentally, praying in a variety of ways is a good technique to expanding interest and desire to pray in the first place.

The practice of justice and service are among the more measurable components because they are things that we engage in outside the normal routine. As we bring the members of our group to

---

[3] *The Religious Dimension of Education in a Catholic School, Guidelines for Reflection and Renewal*, 1988, par. 98.

accept their role in the world as witnesses of the gospel message, we will begin to see them want to do more. We need to allow them opportunities so that they can give expression to their faith in concrete ways, just as their prayer and worship does. With the example of the Church in its social action endeavors and the ideal of the spiritual and corporal works of mercy to guide them, we encourage them to put the Beatitudes into practice in addressing the needs of the poor in our world and, in so doing, to fulfill that which our Lord desires of us. The ways in which we witness our faith are limitless. The call to do so is all-encompassing. Our role is to facilitate the expression of that witness to match the baptismal call of each person to bring others to Christ.

At this point in our journey, we pause for a moment to assess where we are in order to develop a strategy for going farther. Perhaps a break may be needed at this time. Perhaps we need to push farther ahead. Assessing our plan at this point is a necessity. Some will take up the journey again realizing that they are on a lifelong trip, but now they will be traveling with greater purpose. Others may move on to be led by another who will take them further along the way. Some of us may transfer our role of facilitating to someone else and we may become a group member, assuming our new role in the group. Whatever the path we choose, we continue knowing that we have sustenance and protection for the journey from our Divine Master. For His is the kingdom, the power, and the glory, now and forever, Amen!

Chapter 10

The "X" Factor — The Catechist

You are the body of Christ, and each individual is a member. God has appointed some in the church to be, first, apostles, second, prophets, third, teachers, then miracle workers, those with the gift of healing, helpers, administrators, and those with various tongues. Are all members apostles? Are all prophets? Are all teachers? Do all work miracles? Do all have the gift of healing? Can all speak in tongues? Can all interpret tongues? Strive for the greatest gifts.   1 Corinthians 12:27-31

Grace has been given to each of us according to the extent of Christ's gift.... To some the gift he gave was to be apostles, to others it was to be prophets, to others it was to be evangelists, pastors, or teachers. This was to equip the saints for the work of ministry, the building up of the body of Christ, until we all attain to unity of faith and knowledge of the Son of God — to mature manhood, to the extent of Christ's full stature.

Ephesians 4:7, 11-13

The call to teach is like most Divine promptings: it isn't something you can ignore or get away from. The call continues to beckon us until we submit ourselves to its will. It is an honorable calling that, like everything else, has its ups and downs. Realizing that God graces each person with the gifts necessary for their calling, we approach the call with confidence and reassurance (well, maybe not always at first!). It wouldn't be far off the mark to say that teachers are among the most loved groups of people in the world. Teachers impact others far more than they ever realize. It is with this understanding that we look at the roles of each catechist in depth, so that we may comprehend its reach and contemplate its impact.

As "official" teachers of the faith, we are in a unique role among lay ministers. Our place within the Church has always been understood and affirmed. The above Scripture references point out that teachers of the faith have from the very beginning been placed very high among the Church's hierarchy of callings. We are in good company as well. Some of the best minds of the Church were led to teach. In fact, the best and most perfect teacher we have spent His entire life teaching. "Jesus taught. It is the witness that he gives of himself: 'Day after day I sat in the Temple teaching.' It is the admiring observation of the evangelists, surprised to see him teaching everywhere and at all times, teaching in a manner and with an authority previously unknown: 'Crowds gathered to him again; and again, as his custom was, he taught them;' 'and they were astonished at his teaching, for he taught them as one who had authority.' It is also what his enemies note for the purpose of drawing grounds for accusation and condemnation: 'He stirs up the people, teaching throughout all Judea, from Galilee even to this place.'"[1]

---

[1]   *Catechesi Tradendae, On Catechesis in Our Time*, 1979, par. 7.

Even Jesus could not prevent Himself from teaching at all times. How many of us find ourselves falling into a teaching mode at a Sunday barbecue? So our calling is a prompting that comes from God which cannot be suppressed, and one that we accept in fulfillment of our mission in Christ.

The role of the catechist is a very important one in the Church, for "theirs is a particular way of carrying out the promise which the Church makes at every Baptism: to support, pray for, and instruct the baptized and foster their growth in faith."[2] While it is true that our baptismal duty calls every Christian to spread the Gospel, teachers of the faith are given a unique responsibility because the role that catechists perform is of utmost importance in the life of the Church. Catechists are led, and given the gifts, to fulfill the task of explaining, defending, and leading others to a better knowledge and love of their Creator. As daunting as this task is, catechists around the world willingly accept and love their work in Christ. All that we do as Christians should build the kingdom of God. The work we do as teachers of the faith uniquely answers this invitation of God. "Every baptized Catholic is personally called by the Holy Spirit to make his or her contribution to the coming of God's kingdom. Within the lay state there are various vocations, or different spiritual and apostolic roads to be followed by both individuals and groups."[3] The work we do is an intricate part of the mission of Christ. As we participate in the will of God, we put our gifts to use in bringing others to the Lord so that all of humanity comes closer to the kingdom of God.

---

[2]   *Sharing the Light of Faith*, National Catechetical Directory for Catholics of the United States, 1978, par. 213.

[3]   *Guide for Catechists, Document of Vocational, Formative and Promotional Orientation of Catechists in the Territories Dependent on the Congregation for the Evangelization of Peoples*, 1993, par. 2.

Catechists perform their duties faithfully week in and week out. We do our work in the midst of many situations that call for us to persevere no matter what. Often parents, the children's first teachers, are either unschooled in the true doctrines of the Church or hold views which are in conflict with Catholic values. We therefore assume our role in picking up where families leave off, of pointing to the truth in the midst of the manifold deceptions of the world, and of remaining faithful, even in a faithless culture. Throughout all of the challenges we face, catechists press ahead, in spite of all of the factors pulling them away from their true goal. Catechists therefore are the real unsung heroes of contemporary catechesis. "Your work is often lowly and hidden but it is carried out with ardent and generous zeal, and it is an eminent form of the lay apostolate, a form that is particularly important where for various reasons children and young people do not receive suitable religious training in the home. How many of us have received from people like you our first notions of catechism and our preparation for the sacrament of penance, for our first communion and confirmation! The Fourth General Assembly of the Synod did not forget you. I join with it in encouraging you to continue your collaboration in the life of the Church."[4] Wow, what an opinion of the work we do!

As we contemplate the method of bringing others to a mature Christian faith, we must always be mindful that all of our efforts are centered in Christ. It is our love for the faith in Christ that has led us to take on this role of catechesis and so we model our coming to faith upon the natural, gradual human process that God has instilled in each of us. Too often we fall into the "teacher" mode in our religious instruction when we need to remain mindful of our

---

[4] *Catechesi Tradendae, On Catechesis in Our Time*, 1979, par. 66.

role as *catechist*, or sharer of faith. We have frequently used the analogy of journeying with our students. This analogy serves us well as we remember that we are in this for the long haul and not just for the "school year." The journey concept urges us to contemplate each step along the way as an important part of the trip. Furthermore, we are conscious of the place we are traveling toward, which is Christ. "Catechists do not merely instruct their students about Christ; they lead them to him. Consequently, their formation should be inspired by God's own original methodology of faith: his gradual Revelation of the truth that is Christ."[5] We journey each day ever closer to Christ.

If all of this is true, the challenge to the Church and to each of those involved in catechesis is to work to ensure that our catechists are the best they can be. We must all work together to make sure that those who come before us are given the doctrines of the Church in their entirety and with effective methods that allow the Word to be properly sown in their hearts and nurtured. "It is necessary above all to prepare good instructors — parochial catechists, teachers, parents — who are desirous of perfecting themselves in this superior art, which is indispensable and requires religious instruction."[6] Our students deserve the best, and so do we. By working to make ourselves the most prepared and knowledgeable people we can be, we are more able to allow this to happen. In helping catechists know their faith and by perfecting methods for sharing it, the Church continues to fulfill its vocation to make disciples of all nations. To the extent that we remain open to new ways to pass on our faith, we as catechists participate in the role of Christians

[5]   *National Directory for Catechesis*, 2005, page 241.
[6]   *On Evangelization in the Modern World, Evangelii Nuntiandi*, 1975, par. 44.

down through the ages. How can we do this? What does this look like? These are the questions we hope to clarify in this chapter.

The catechist should be someone who already practices a faithful life within the Church. "Catechists need to be practicing Catholics who participate fully in the communal worship and life of the Church and who have been prepared for their apostolate by appropriate catechetical training. Their commissioning by the Church is a participation in the divine calling to teach as Jesus did. Their personal relationship with Jesus Christ energizes their service to the Church and provides the continuing motivation, vitality, and force of their catechetical activity. Christ invites all catechists to follow him as a teacher of the faith and witness to the truth of the faith."[7] We therefore call people of healthy faith lives to share their experiences and love of Christ with others who are journeying as well. Our experiences help to guide others just as a jungle guide uses his experiences to assist other jungle travelers.

Since a large part of the work we do is witnessing our faith to others, the practice of this faith should be one that is a healthy example for all to see. This isn't meant to slight others or to imply that they are called to a lesser degree of holiness. It is simply an expression of the high level of dignity and competence that the Church holds for its teachers of the faith. "The Church, as it always does, asks much from its catechists.... It asks that they be women and men of faith, filled with the spirit of the gospel, able to lead the community in prayer and free to encourage the community to serve those who are in need. It presumes that they are people of prayer, not only of private prayer but also the world of ritual, bodily prayer."[8]

---

[7] *National Directory for Catechesis*, 2005, pages 228-229.

[8] *The Catechetical Documents*, Anne Marie Mongoven, OP, Overview of *The Rite of Christian Initiation of Adults*, 1996, p. 421.

Now that we know the nature of our call, the expectation of the Church and parents toward the work we do, and realize the level of training we are expected to have, each of us as catechists must take on these expectations with the same enthusiasm we take on each new year as we gather together with our students who are eager to hear the Word of God. "Catechists and religion teachers hold a central role within the ministry of adolescent catechesis, second only to parents. They are formally involved in an actual learning setting with youth, sponsoring them in their journey to maturity in Catholic Christian faith…. The Church calls catechists/religion teachers to work toward developing the following competencies, recognizing that growth as a catechist/religion teacher is an ongoing process."[9]

As we assume this aspect of our calling, let us never lose sight of the reason that we call catechists to such a high level of competency. The people we seek to evangelize and catechize deserve to receive the faith from people of great enthusiasm, knowledge and methods. They are entitled to quality instruction because the message is vitally important to their salvation and the love with which we share it should inspire them in turn to love as Jesus did. "And may the world of our time, which is searching, sometimes with anguish, sometimes with hope, be enabled to receive the Good News not from evangelizers who are dejected, discouraged, impatient or anxious, but from ministers of the Gospel whose lives glow with fervor, who have first received the joy of Christ, and who are willing to risk their lives so that the Kingdom may be proclaimed and the Church established in the midst of the world."[10]

The catechist personally impacts the transfer of information

---

[9] *The Challenge of Adolescent Catechesis: Maturing in Faith*, 1986, par. 44.

[10] *On Evangelization in the Modern World, Evangelii Nuntiandi*, 1975, par. 80.

at least as much as any textbook does. Textbooks, audio or visual aids, various kinesthetic learning tools and curriculum guides are tools of the trade. For any tool to be applied correctly, the person using it should master its use and know when which tool is best suited to which application. As we study the art of catechesis, each of us should assess our strengths and weaknesses, hone our skills, and continually increase our knowledge to assure the best means of handing on the Christian faith. While all of this sounds a bit overwhelming, it is something that is acquired little by little over a long period of time. Just as Jesus grew in wisdom, so must we. Just as Jesus sat at the feet of the teachers of the faith, so must we learn from other skilled people. In the catechetical document *Sharing the Light of Faith*, the National Catechetical Directory for Catholics of the United States, our bishops outline several guidelines concerning revelation and faith which catechists are urged to employ in their work of sharing the faith:

> — "Catechists should draw upon all the sources: biblical, liturgical, ecclesial, and natural.
> — Catechists should note the historical character of revelation and faith.
> — Catechists need to understand the development of doctrine.
> — Catechists situate catechesis within the community of believers.
> — Catechists pray for the discernment of the Spirit.
> — Catechists emphasize God's living presence.
> — Catechists give guidance on private revelation."[11]

---

[11] *Sharing the Light of Faith*, National Catechetical Directory for Catholics of the United States, 1978, par. 60.

Furthermore, the National Catechetical Directory outlines several qualities that are inherent in the ideal catechist. These qualities are ones that the catechist should develop within themselves to help them become better witnesses to those whom they try to bring to fullness of faith. These are:

— The call to an ideal and recognition of a challenge.
— A response to a call by God and the Church.
— A witness to the Gospels.
— A commitment to the Church.
— A sharer in community.
— A servant of the community.
— Has knowledge, skills, and abilities.[12]

Another list that is helpful in assessing and developing ourselves as catechists comes from the document *Challenge of Adolescent Catechesis: Maturing in Faith.* In this document, our bishops give a brief description of the skills and abilities that each catechist should develop:

"The catechist/religion teacher demonstrates the ability to do the following:

— design and conduct learning experiences for youth, utilizing a variety of learning processes, media, methods, and resources;
— relate the Gospel to the world of youth in the language, signs, symbols, and images understandable to youth;
— utilize communication, group discussion, community

---

[12] Cf. *Sharing the Light of Faith*, National Catechetical Directory for Catholics of the United States, 1978, par. 205-211.

building, faith-sharing, and storytelling processes and
skills;
— design and conduct worship, prayer, justice, and service
experiences with youth."[13]

As we attempt to form the faith of those under us, we continue with our own faith formation as well. Since the impact we
have on those around us is so important to how our message is received, we must always be guided by the Holy Spirit as we form
ourselves to be more and more Christ-like. This is true, of course,
for every Christian but most especially for catechists. Our formation must lead to ever greater commitment to Christ and to His
mission. As such, it requires that we continually conform ourselves
to the way of Christ. "Today, perhaps more than ever before, it is
important to recognize that learning is a lifelong experience.... This
is necessary for adults to function efficiently, but more important,
to achieve full realization of their potential as persons whose destiny includes but also transcends this life."[14] This isn't something
that we should take lightly. The example we give others in forming ourselves is exactly the lesson we teach everyday. If we show
others that faith formation is important to us, they will think it important for themselves as well. We teach by our example more
forcefully than we do with our words. As we seek to bring others
to know, love and serve God and others, we must ensure that this
is a goal we are working towards ourselves in our own lives.

People who seek to instruct others in this area must themselves
be people of character. We cannot overstate the importance for
catechists and other sharers of the faith to be true witnesses of

---

[13] *The Challenge of Adolescent Catechesis: Maturing in Faith*, 1986, par. 45.
[14] *To Teach as Jesus Did*, A Pastoral Message on Catholic Education, 1972, par. 43.

Christ. People easily see through false facades. When we engage in teaching something which we do not personally practice, it impacts negatively the message we are trying to convey. We must therefore show others that what we say is what we mean, and how we live our lives is reflected by this. "It is often said nowadays that the present century thirsts for authenticity. Especially in regard to young people it is said that they have a horror of the artificial or false and that they are searching above all for truth and honesty. These 'signs of the times' should find us vigilant. Either tacitly or aloud — but always forcefully — we are being asked: Do you really believe what you are proclaiming? Do you live what you believe? Do you really preach what you live? The witness of life has become more than ever an essential condition for real effectiveness in preaching. Precisely because of this we are, to a certain extent, responsible for the progress of the gospel that we proclaim."[15] The age-old cliché is true: "Practice what you preach!"

Since catechesis demands that we share our faith stories and relate all of our teachings to everyday life, we must always be looking at the world through the eyes of the sacramental principle described earlier in this book. By allowing ourselves to see God in His created world we become a sacramental people. Just as sacraments point to a reality beneath their surface, we point to the reality of God and His love mysteriously hidden in all that we are and do. While we work to create a method of catechesis that allows us to better share our message, the person of the catechist does much to influence the personal acceptance of this message by all of the members of the group. "No method, not even one much proved in use, frees the catechist from the personal task of assimilating and

---

[15] *On Evangelization in the Modern World, Evangelii Nuntiandi*, 1975, par. 76.

passing judgment on the concrete circumstances, and from some adjustment to them. For outstanding human and Christian qualities in the catechists will be able to do more to produce successes than will the methods selected."[16]

In this chapter we have attempted to look at the intangibles associated with sharing the light of faith. The most influential intangible is the person of the catechist. By forming ourselves in the faith, we as catechists (and others) allow the faith to be "caught," and not taught. We do not do this in a vacuum; the whole community must work to assist in this endeavor. "Catechesis, finally, demands the witness of faith, both from the catechists and from the ecclesial community, a witness that is joined to an authentic example of the Christian life and to a readiness for sacrifice (cf. LG, 12, 17; NA, 2)."[17] As we witness the love of God, our stories witness to the young Christians we seek to form. By living the gospel message, we ensure that our faith becomes the faith of the Church, which in turn becomes the faith of the world. May God bless you as you follow in His footsteps.

---

[16] *General Catechetical Directory*, Sacred Congregation for the Clergy, 1971, par. 71.

[17] *General Catechetical Directory*, Sacred Congregation for the Clergy, 1971, par. 35.

Chapter 11

The "Y" Factor
— The Students
and Their
Questions

Now when a large crowd had gathered, including people
who had come to him from every city, he said in a parable, "The sower went out to sow his seed. And as he
sowed some fell along the footpath, and it was trampled
underfoot and the birds of the sky ate it up. And other
seed fell on rock, and when it grew up it was scorched
because it had no moisture. And other seed fell among
the thorns, and when the thorns grew up with it they
choked it. And other seed fell on the good earth, and
when it grew up it gave fruit a hundredfold." After he
had said these things he cried out, "Whoever has ears
to hear, let them hear!" His disciples asked him what
this parable could mean. "To you it's given to know the
mysteries of the Kingdom of God," he said, "but to the
rest of them it's given in parables, so that seeing they
may not see, and hearing they may not understand. This
is the parable. The seed is the word of God. Those on
the footpath are those who hear, and then the Devil

comes and snatches the word from their heart, so they
won't believe and be saved. Those on the rock are those
who, when they hear, accept the word joyfully, yet these
have no root; they believe for a time but forsake the word
in time of trial. Now the seed that fell among the thorns,
these are those who hear but are choked by the worries
and wealth and pleasures of life as they proceed, and
they don't mature. But the seed on the good earth, these
are those who listen to the word with an honest and good
heart, hold fast to it, and bear fruit with perseverance."

Luke 8:4-15

Who will harm you if you're zealous for what's right?
But even if you do suffer for what's right, you're
blessed! Have no fear of them and don't be frightened,
but in your hearts revere Christ as the Lord. Always be
ready with a reply for anyone who demands an explanation for the hope you have within you, but do it hum-
bly and respectfully and have a clean conscience, so that
when people malign your good behavior in Christ they'll
be put to shame.   1 Peter 3:13-16

Jesus loved to teach. He loved to take a message to His listeners in such a way that it left them dwelling on what He said for
a long time afterward. We are still contemplating His teachings!
So when Jesus had a message to give, He tried to pass it along in
such a way as to be pertinent to each person in a manner they could
understand. Even Jesus realized you had to partner the message with
an effective method! Jesus' teachings usually led to questions by
the hearers of His message. Sometimes these questions were even
from His disciples. But Jesus knew that the questions would come,

and He always had an appropriate answer. Sometimes He even got questions that were, say, tricky. Some of these were people asking questions for the worst of reasons. But some were probing His thoughts for other, less cynical reasons. We have our own "clumsy questioners," don't we?

If you teach long enough, you will come across the person who fits the description of the "class clown." These are the people whose job it is to do anything to make people giggle. They accept this task with eagerness knowing there is a certain price to pay, but the laughs are worth the punishment. It is these people that many teachers fear the most; the heckler in the back row or the child who asks questions veiled with humor. Initially, this person is no fun to deal with, but perhaps we can look at it from a different perspective. When people ask questions they are engaging their thinking capacities. By hearing something, processing it and formulating a question based upon what they have heard, they show that there is a higher level of thinking going on. Think about it. If our students come up with questions that are meant to make fun of the topic or the presenter or for any other reason, they have sufficiently internalized the material to come up with a question that is at least somewhat pertinent to the topic. As a start, this may be enough.

Often, our first reaction is to dismiss the antics as child's play or disrespect. However, when we begin to understand the culture from which our groups are coming, we may well conclude that the question might contain an element of truth that needs exploring. By latching on to the situation and addressing the question with humor, we will engage the minds of all the students while affirming the person who has asked it. When Jesus got His "trick questions," His response was thoughtful, thought-provoking, and filled with the wisdom of God. Whenever we face the questions of our students, we must follow the example of Jesus. We must see the questions for what they are, then we must speak the truth in love, just as Christ would do. When we do this, we uphold the value of the person without validating the silliness of the question. We also take our questioners to a place they never expected. In this way we relate the message of the Gospel to everyday life. We must therefore "always be ready to give an explanation to anyone who asks us."

Jesus often taught in parables. His teaching was meant to give the essence of a vital message in a way that the listeners could understand and make their own. When we share Scripture with our students, we must always be ready to put it into the context of their daily lives. When we do this we make the message pertinent to each one where they live. Our goal is to encourage each member of the group to actively participate in what we are doing so that the faith we share becomes a faith they own. "Christian education is intended to 'make men's faith become living, conscious, and active, through the light of instruction' (CD, 14)."[1] As our students begin to question their faith, they will try to validate the beliefs they hold. We must guide them to do this in a healthy and safe manner, leading them to investigate their questions and to find answers for the yearnings of their soul. This is a good and useful way of expending our energies in the classroom.

When we see them actively engaged, we know we are headed in the right direction. It is through this active participation that they will come to gradually accept and make a part of themselves that which they have heard. "God's Word when proclaimed, celebrated, shared, and lived in the Christian community is dynamic and fruitful. What an opportunity exists when the energy and giftedness of young people can be engaged with the vibrancy and richness of

---

[1] *To Teach as Jesus Did*, A Pastoral Message on Catholic Education, 1972, par. 102.

God's Word! The possibilities for personal development and growth in faith are then enormous and can lead to a richer life for the entire Catholic Christian community and for the family. The enthusiasm and challenge offered by young people who become more involved in the life of the Church can energize parish, home, and society."[2]

By engaging our group in the learning process each day, we will ensure that the seeds of the Gospel message are being planted in the garden soil of each person's soul. To help the seeds grow we must cultivate them carefully so that they take root and are thereafter properly nourished. While there are some factors that are beyond our control, we realize that those aspects which we can control should be given our best efforts. As we engage our students in the life of Christ, we seek to provide those opportunities that help us best infuse the Gospel message. The experiential method of teaching has been shown to help students retain more information than any other. Experiential teaching, or active learning, is the one that fully engages a person by allowing them to do more on their own. By experiencing the lesson in actual practice, students are able to make the lesson a part of themselves. As we use this method in catechesis, it is important to relate every experience to our faith lives. "Experience is of great importance in catechesis.... Experience can... increase the intelligibility of the Christian message, by providing illustrations and examples which shed light on the truths of revelation. At the same time, experience itself should be interpreted in the light of revelation."[3]

---

[2] *The Challenge of Adolescent Catechesis: Maturing in Faith*, 1986, par. 4.

[3] *Sharing the Light of Faith*, National Catechetical Directory for Catholics of the United States, 1978, par. 176.

As we look to provide opportunities for our groups to better acclimate themselves to our message, we will find ourselves searching for a variety of ways to pass along our message that fits the learning styles of each individual. These differing methods will vary by the makeup of the group and the dynamics within these groups. By gearing our methods to each specific group, we further our ability to pass along a message that will take root because it speaks to the heart and soul of each individual person. "The age and the intellectual development of Christians, their degree of ecclesial and spiritual maturity and many other personal circumstances demand that catechesis should adopt widely differing methods for the attainment of its specific aim: education in the faith."[4]

All of this is certainly not an easy task. However, this is a worthwhile endeavor because we know that true happiness here and hereafter lies at the core of the Christian message. Our motivation should be the satisfaction that we are bringing others to Christ. The task is a difficult one, but if we put forth our best efforts, we will more effectively live and share the gospel message as God intends. "The opportunity of engaging adolescents in the life of the Church challenges us. As youth experience and express their expanding freedom, they resist mediocre or halfhearted efforts. Effective catechesis with youth requires that the adult members of our community grow continually in their faith and in their ability to share it with others."[5] This is true for all people sharing the faith. Adults are just as demanding of their teachers of the faith as our young people are. Therefore, as we guide our groups to a deeper understanding of God's love and the happiness He wishes to share, we

---

[4] *Catechesi Tradendae, On Catechesis in Our Time*, 1979, par. 51.

[5] *The Challenge of Adolescent Catechesis: Maturing in Faith*, 1986, par. 4.

will find ourselves working ever harder to fulfill our call in Christ. Thus do we participate with God in sharing the Good News to a searching people. Our reward is the satisfaction of knowing that perhaps we have planted a seed that may one day blossom into an active, vibrant faith, a faith that is on fire for Christ.

If we have done our part in this process, if we have prepared the soil and planted the seeds properly, we will begin to see the fruits of our efforts and be ready to turn over the faith that is being developed to the people who are embracing it. As they learn to deal with their own questions, they will forge their faith into a system that they will rely upon their entire lives. Our ultimate goal is eternal happiness for ourselves and our students in the loving embrace of Christ. As we learn to love better, we grow closer to this goal with each step all along the way.

"Faith often needs to be personally held and critically appropriated. As we hand on the Catholic Christian tradition and discern the activity of God in the contemporary pluralistic and secular world and in young people's own experience, we invite them to find a vocabulary to articulate their belief, to examine it, and to own it. We invite them to think for themselves, to come to their own 'faith knowing.' We encourage them to critically reflect upon their own experience and to allow the wisdom of Scripture and tradition to inform and transform their lives."[6] Our faith is one that offers true freedom of acceptance. As we allow people to come to a personally-held acceptance of the Christian life, we pass on to them the gift of faith as God intended. We cannot force others to believe. We cannot force anyone to love. The best we can do is lead others to a place where a free and conscious acceptance is possible. In

---

[6]   *The Challenge of Adolescent Catechesis: Maturing in Faith*, 1986, par. 23.

order for this to happen, we must meet our travelers where they are. The Comprehensive Catechetical model outlined in this book offers the best opportunity for this to develop. By working through each step in the process, Christians who are being formed are given the fullness of the Christian message in a manner that is accessible and understandable in a personal way. I cannot imagine that Christ would ask for anything more.

Our students, young and old, approach us with a spiritual yearning for fulfillment. We embrace them along their journey and walk with them. Eventually they begin to walk on their own, apart from us, albeit with some assistance. They seek to own their faith. Although their struggles will be a challenge, they will gain strength in each obstacle overcome. Our questions about God and faith are our way of growing. If we are willing and prepared to help answer these questions, our fellow pilgrims, and we, will be strengthened on our journey. All of us seek to grow in faith. Hopefully our seed will fall on rich soil and we will be among those who "have heard the word, embraced it with a generous and good heart, and bore fruit through perseverance." May God work through our gardens of faith and may He provide all we need to bear hearty fruit.

Chapter 12

The Alpha and the Omega — To Know, to Love, to Serve

Then I saw a new heaven and a new earth — the first heaven and the first earth had passed away and the sea was no more. And I saw the holy city, new Jerusalem, coming down out of Heaven from God, prepared as a bride is adorned for her husband. Then I heard a loud voice from the throne say, "Behold, God's dwelling is now with men. He shall dwell with them and they shall be His people, and God Himself will be with them. He'll wipe every tear from their eyes and death shall be no more — no more grief or crying or pain, for what came before has passed away." Then the One seated on the throne said, "Behold, I'll make all things new!" He also said, "Write this down, for these words are trustworthy and true." Then He said to me, "It is finished! I am the Alpha and the Omega, the beginning and the end. Those who thirst I'll allow to drink freely from the spring of living water. Whoever is victorious shall inherit all these things, and I shall be his God and he shall be My son."

Revelation 21:1-7

If we were to throw out all of the lesson plans, textbooks, curriculum guides and previous experiences in any of our Christian formation programs, how would we begin again? Where would we start from? What elements would be most important? As we step back and survey the landscape of the methods we employ to form Christians, we begin to realize that our goal is usually much simpler than we make it out to be. As we summarize the Scriptures, especially the teachings of Jesus, we begin to understand that God's plan is a simple, yet profound one. God wishes to draw all people to Himself. He wishes all people to be happy, not in an earthly sense, which is temporary, but in a heavenly, eternal way. Since God created us, He knows exactly what we desire and need to be eternally happy. As we come to the final chapter of this book, we step back and see our work as a participation in the plan of God. Where does God, and therefore we, want to take our fellow pilgrims?

As discussed earlier in this book, we begin building a relationship with God by casually knowing Him and His message. As we deepen the relationship, our knowledge helps us grow in our love of God, which in turn leads us to a desire to serve Him as well. We seek to engage our head, heart and hands in this endeavor. As we complete our work on the Comprehensive Catechetical model, we want to urge all catechists and adult facilitators everywhere toward the end goal of our spiritual journey. "Why did God make you?" "God made me to know Him, to love Him, and to serve Him in this world, and to be happy with Him for ever in heaven."[1] The entire Comprehensive Catechetical model is encompassed in this formula, every historical educational model is contained within this statement, and all of the teachings of the Scriptures, both Old and

---

[1]   *Baltimore Catechism*, Part 1, Lesson 1, Question 6.

New are captured in this one assertion. This concept will please our older Catholics because it is straight out of the *Baltimore Catechism*. And yet, our objective is truly that simple. Once we realize this, everything we do to lead others to Christian maturity takes on a clearer and more precise objective.

To say that our true goal in catechesis of both youth and adults is to bring people to know, love and serve God and others so that we can achieve eternal happiness is to declare that all of us have the same purpose in life. We are all headed to the same place and will receive the same reward. Obviously, we all have a different role to play in getting to this point, but the message and method for all of us is the same.

Comprehensive Catechesis places this idealistic goal into a plan that is easily implemented in any group, in any parish, in any circumstance. To "know something" means we must be instructed in a way that allows the message to be comprehended and connected with our own life experiences. To "love something" means that we come to know something enough that we make a conscious decision to allow it to become a part of our lives in the form of a much greater commitment. To know and to love lead us to want to serve as we willingly choose to give of ourselves. We are led to a desire to serve because our understanding (knowledge) and appreciation (love) cause us to want to ensure the best for whatever we know and love. This is true for anything that we value whether it be another person, an object, or a hobby. The more we know and love something, the more we wish to ensure its presence in our lives for an extended period of time. In so doing, we realize the importance of striking a balance between intellect and emotion, knowing and loving. Message and method must likewise be balanced. As we work toward our goal we must be ever conscious of why we do what we do.

Contemporary religious education models need to be re-worked so that they are more holistic and experiential. This doesn't mean that we must abandon all legitimate forms of catechesis. We need to build upon that which helps us achieve our goal and add other components that complement them. Through all of the work we do, we must continually seek to bring others to a more complete understanding of the gospel message. "Merely 'teaching about' religion is not enough. Instead such programs must strive to teach doctrine fully, foster community, and prepare their students for Christian service. Whether it takes place in a Catholic school or not, it is essential that the Catholic community offer children and young people an experience of catechesis which indeed gives 'clarity and vigor' to faith, fosters living in the spirit of Christ, encourages participation in the liturgy and sacraments, and motivates involvement in the apostolate (GE, 4)."[2] We want to make our students well-balanced in their approach to God. We want to bring them to a healthy love and knowledge of their Creator who longs to share His love with them. "It is also one of the aims of catechesis to give young catechumens the simple but solid certainties that will help them to seek to know the Lord more and better."[3] This knowing helps them make a full and conscious decision to love and serve. All of this can only be done by someone who has previously come to know, love and is now serving the one true God. It is this sharing of our light of faith that brings others willingly to God. It is the fire of our love of God that illuminates the way for others to follow. Finally, in the sharing of our love for God through others, we express our love in a tangible way that others can readily see and embrace.

---

[2]   *To Teach as Jesus Did*, A Pastoral Message on Catholic Education, 1972, par. 87.

[3]   *Catechesi Tradendae, On Catechesis in Our Time*, 1979, par. 60.

Earlier in this book we shared the concept of the growth of a mature Christian. As human beings we begin as dependent persons, become independent and are called to be inter-dependent as true Christians living the way of Jesus. By helping others through these stages, we allow them to make a thoughtful decision to follow in the footsteps of Christ. As this relationship with God deepens over time, each person renews his or her decision over and over again growing closer and closer to the Creator. "As an evangelizing activity, catechesis promotes an ongoing conversion toward a permanent commitment to the Lord."[4]

We step back and contemplate our role in building the Kingdom of God. Our task is that of bringing others to know, love and serve God and others so that we and they can be happy with Him forever in heaven. Our next logical question is "Why?" Just as our students ask us — and we should therefore ask ourselves the question "So what?" — we now ask ourselves "Why is this principle true? Why has God created us? Why does God desire us to be with Him? Why does serving each other show love for God?" Perhaps the explanation of this concept comes from our understanding of relationships, especially the relationship of God and His people.

Often we compare the love of God and His Church with the love of a couple in marriage. The relationships begin and are fostered in the much same ways, as an earlier chapter relates. But let's take this comparison to a deeper level. If one of the ultimate expressions of love in a marriage is the propagation of children, this would also hold true for God. God is love and as He created this world, one of the ultimate expressions of His love would be the creation of children. And so we were made, out of love, to share

---

[4]   *The Challenge of Adolescent Catechesis: Maturing in Faith*, 1986, par. 9.

His love. We are expressions of God's love. Just as children are brought up in love so that they may one day share their love with another, we are reared in love so that we may come to know, love and share our love with others in Christ.

We are God's children. When we live this way, we create the world God envisions. When we grow to know, love and serve each other, we serve God in the process. By following in the footsteps of Christ we become the "Church" which was formed by Jesus upon the rock of Peter, and the small community Jesus first formed. When we build a community of support and love, we are Church. When we grow together in our understanding of the Scriptures and awareness of God in our everyday lives, we are Church. When our hearts burn to know and love God more in our study of the faith as a people of God, we are Church. When we gather to express our faith through prayer and worship, we are Church. When we willingly accept and live out our baptismal duty to show our love of God through others, we are Church. Our faith encompasses our whole being: body, mind, soul, and strength. By bringing others to this understanding, we are doing the most important work in the world. Our calling to do so is divinely inspired. As we live and share our faith, we become Christ-like. As we engage our head, heart and hands, we become the instruments through which God works. May God, in His infinite glory, bless us as we allow Him to work through us. May the work we do bring others a little closer to Christ, for it is "through Him, with Him, and in Him, in the unity of the Holy Spirit, that all glory and honor is yours, almighty Father, for ever and ever. AMEN!" (Adapted from Romans 11:36).

Other Resources

The Catechetical Documents. Chicago, Illinois: Liturgy Training
Publications, 1996.

The Introduction from the English translation of the *Rite of Christian
Initiation of Adults.* International Committee on English in the
Liturgy, Inc., 1985.

The *General Catechetical Directory.* Libreria Editrice Vaticana, 1971.

Adult Catechesis in the Christian Community. Libreria Editrice
Vaticana, 1990.

The Challenge of Adolescent Catechesis: Maturing in Faith. Washington, D.C. National Federation for Catholic Youth Ministry,
Inc., 1986.

Basic Teachings for Catholic Religious Education. Washington, D.C.
United States Catholic Conference, 1973.

Guidelines for Doctrinally Sound Catechetical Materials. Washington,
D.C. United States Catholic Conference, 1991.

*Sharing the Light of Faith: National Catechetical Directory for
Catholics of the United States.* Washington, D.C. United
States Catholic Conference, 1979.

To Teach as Jesus Did. Washington, D.C. United States Catholic
Conference, 1972.

The Guide for Catechists. Vatican City. Congregation for the Evangelization of Peoples, 1993.

The Religious Dimension of Education in a Catholic School. Vatican
City. Congregation for Catholic Education, 1988.

Apostolic exhortation of Pope John Paul II. *On Catechesis in Our Time
(Catechesi Tradendae).* United States Catholic Conference,
1979.

Apostolic exhortation of Pope Paul VI. *On Evangelization in the Modern World* (*Evangelii Nuntiandi*). United States Catholic Conference, 1975.

English translation of the *Catechism of the Catholic Church* for the United States of America. United States Catholic Conference, Inc., 1997.

New American Bible with Revised New Testament. Washington, D.C. Confraternity of Christian Doctrine, 1991.

Boucher, Therese M. *Evangelizing Unchurched Children*. San Jose, California: Resource Publications, Inc., 2000.

Prayer for Catechists

Dear God,
You are the Father of Truth.
As we search for ways to
know, love and serve You better
may we always be guided by Your Word.
We pray that Your Church upon Earth
will mirror the love of Your Holy Trinity.
We pray for all people of faith,
their families,
their catechists,
their pastors and bishops;
that all people will come to
a mature Christian faith.
We pray for our world,
that You will bring us
ever closer to Your kingdom.
Finally, we ask for Your blessing upon us.
As we work to share our love for You,
may we be blessed with a strong faith,
a powerful life of prayer,
and a desire to always bring people to You.
May we be granted this through the name of
Your Son, Jesus Christ.
Amen.

ST PAULS

This book was produced by St. Pauls/Alba House, the Society of St. Paul, an international religious congregation of priests and brothers dedicated to serving the Church through the communications media.

For information regarding this and associated ministries of the Pauline Family of Congregations, write to the Vocation Director, Society of St. Paul, P.O. Box 189, 9531 Akron-Canfield Road, Canfield, Ohio 44406-0189. Phone (330) 702-0396; or E-mail: spvocationoffice@aol.com or check our internet site, www.albahouse.org